Workbook on

SALES and Closing Deals

The Essential Sales Guide for

Consultants, Speakers, Authors, and Experts

By Wael Badawy, PhD

Win Your Brand

100 - 111 5th Ave SW -Suite 337, Calgary, AB, T2P 3Y6

http://www.WinYourBrand.com

Ordering Information:

Quantity sales. Special discounts are available on quantity purchases by corporations, associations, and others. For details, contact the publisher at the address above.

Orders by trade bookstores and wholesalers. Please contact Big Distribution:

Tel: (403) 907-0907;

Fax: (403) 547-4555 or visit www.WinYourBrand.com

Printed in Canada

Publisher's Cataloging-in-Publication data

Badawy, Wael. SALES and Closing Deals – The Workbook / Wael Badawy.

ISBN 978-1-989040-01-0 Electronic book

978-1-989040-00-3 Paperback

1. The main category of the book —Business —

First Edition. revised

Table of Contents

DEDICATION

To the love of my life Roya

and to my children Saif, Seleem, Adam and Zain

without whom this book would have

been completed SIX years earlier.

To my Mother, Sister and late Father who believed in me and inspired me to be who I am.

ACKNOWLEDGMENTS

First and foremost, I would dedicate this book to my wife Roya.

also thank my wonderful wife for the allowing me to spend much time in front of my computer.

I'd like to thank my parents for future gatherings as I'm sure they will all read it soon.

My business partners, especially to continue on in the Journey.

I thank each of them for the community they've created!

Thanks for everything.

Thanks to the general community for using my concepts and providing great ideas and support via mailing lists; without this help I could not create newsletters and podcasts.

How to Use this Manual

Do...

- Read it from cover to cover
- Dip into it whenever you have a spare moment
- Keep it on your Desktop or Laptop
- Note your sales "wins" within its pages
- Memorise your favourite answers
- Find yourself adopting the beliefs and living the life of a Sales Superstar
- Use it as a resource for creative 10 minute energisers in sales meetings and trainings
- Buy copies for the whole of your sales team
- Tell your friends about it
- Use it as the secret of your success!

Top 10 Tips of Sales Superstars

1 No objection has any meaning other than the meaning which you give to it

2 Always be 100% responsible for the outcome of every client interaction

3 Always remain calm in the face of client objections

4 No-one has the power to make you feel bad unless you let them

5 Dealing with objections is simply part of selling

6 Dealing with objections expertly will set you apart from mere average salespeople

7 Modelling successful salespeople and studying books and audio products is part of being at the top of your game

8 Write down every objection you can think of, plan your answers and practice them until you are fluent in the use of them

9 Constantly revise and improve your objection handling techniques

10 Believe in yourself, your product / service and the sales profession

When You Become an Expert Objection Handler...

You will:

- Build better rapport with clients
- Stay more focused on your sales objectives
- Remain on calls longer
- Be less stressed
- Feel great about your chosen profession
- Enjoy the sales process much more
- Avoid confrontation with clients
- Be more persuasive
- Become a master of communicating in difficult situations
- Portray professionalism, confidence and client focus
- Prevent most objections ever happening!
- Make more sales at higher fees!

And in the Beginning there was Feel, Felt, Found

FEEL I understand the way that you feel

FELT Other people felt that way too!

FOUND However, what they found was ...

Answer objection!

Strengths

- Easy to use and remember
- Adaptable

Weaknesses

- No good for complaints or personal objections (e.g. *"I don't like you!"*)
- Can't be used over and over for multiple objections

Sales Superstar says...

"Consider your most common objections and plan and personalise your Feel / Felt / Found answers with real life examples and statistics."

"I understand how you feel John. When I worked with (name client) they felt that the initial investment was outside of their budget too. After implementing WinYourBrand coaching programmes across their organisation they found that their sales rose by 45% which represents a 275% return on investment. This equates to a bottom line profit figure of ... (name figure)."

Practise now!

Top 10 Tips for Dealing with Objections

1 Take your time

2 Clarify the objection

3 Don't waffle

4 Choose your words carefully

5 Take a deep breath

6 Watch the pace of your speech

7 Listen! Listen! Listen!

8 Answer the right objection

9 Ask a question

10 Remember that you cannot lose what you haven't got!

Voice Coaching and Making an Impact

Control of the voice and its qualities is outside of most people's conscious awareness most of the time. For this reason it is an area of study that gets little attention in most sales training. This is unfortunate because, as we all know, it's not what you say it's the way that you say it. It's therefore essential that you master this important sales and life skill.

Pace. Keep your pace steady and controlled. This shows professionalism and seniority sending the message that you are listening and that you are considering what the client has to say! Ironically, most of us have a tendency under pressure to rush, which sends completely the opposite message.

Tone is simply the expression of feelings in your voice i.e. confident, happy, knowledgeable, dynamic etc. Consider how you want to come over on your calls. The component parts of your tone should be flexible to each and every client and each and every situation. The way to convey a tone is to "do" the feeling.

Pitch is the note that your voice is on – high or low. This is particularly useful in relationship to the ends of sentences. Try saying out loud, *"You've probably heard of us"* but concentrate on keeping a level pitch at the end of the sentence. As you listen to it you will hear that this is a statement. Now try the same statement but going down at the end of the sentence. You will hear that this is an order. Now try going up at the end of the sentence. This sounds like a question.

Many salespeople go up under pressure and invite objections by sounding like they are asking a question! Conversely, using the downward or order tone can be incredibly powerful for controlling conversations.

Practice. Whilst all of this sounds very simple; in practice you will have habitual patterns of speech that you may find very difficult to change. It can also be very difficult to even identify your own voice patterns as you often don't hear yourself the same way as everyone else does. I would highly recommend getting others to listen to and critique your calls, focusing on these elements that we have discussed.

Judge by results. Because the non-verbal elements of the call are mostly outside of conscious awareness this means that when you do perfect these skills you will add that magical element to your answers. This will increase not only your sales results but also your ability to build rapport with your clients.

For more on this subject why not listen to one of my audio products or attend one of my seminars.

First Things First

You are about to learn the most effective closing techniques ever discovered. Before we start talking about the closes, I'd like to talk about the antecedents to closing. One of Murphy's Laws is that "before you do anything, you have to do something else first."

Before you close the sale, you have to do several other things first. Here are the two psychological antecedents to closing. You must know and use these if you want to be effective.

The first requirement, which you've heard a thousand times, is enthusiasm. ***51% of all closing effectiveness comes from your enthusiasm***, your excitement about your product or service. One of the best definitions I ever heard of closing is that it is a "transfer of enthusiasm." In other words, when you successfully transfer your enthusiasm about your product or service into the mind of the prospect, he or she will buy and a sale takes place.

Believe In What You Sell

It is essential that you have enough enthusiasm to transfer a sufficient amount into the mind of the other person. What this means is that the most effective sales people know their product, they believe in their product, and love their product. They really believe that their product has very worthwhile benefits for their customer.

If you don't believe in your product, if you don't love your product, if you wouldn't use it yourself, if you wouldn't sell it to your best friend or your mother, then you're probably selling the wrong product.

Without this deep belief in the goodness of what you're selling, you can never reach that level of enthusiasm that must be transferred into the mind of the prospect to make them want to buy.

By the way, I don't mean the "rah! rah!" jumping around type of enthusiasm. I mean what is called constrained enthusiasm. This is when your enthusiasm is kept inside; you like a kettle, a boiling kettle with the lid put on it so that you literally shine with enthusiasm. You seem to have a dynamic tension, an excitement about you, but it isn't in how fast you talk or how quickly you move. It's contained within.

—————————————

YOUR NOTES

Your Source of Power

Constrained enthusiasm has one of the most powerful effects of all on other people, more than you can imagine. Ralph Waldo Emerson said, "Nothing great was ever accomplished without enthusiasm."

——————————————

YOUR NOTES

Expect the Best

The second psychological quality you require is confident expectations. You must confidently expect that the person is going to say "yes" if you just ask often enough. When you ask the prospect to buy, you must confidently expect them to buy.

For example, you ask expectantly, "Would you like the red one or the green one today?" In other words, you don't ask, "Are you going to take one or not?" or "Is this what you had mind?" Instead, you ask for the sale expectantly, and the more confidently you expect to sell, the more likely it is that you will sell.

Confidence in selling comes from knowledge, it comes from practice, it comes from experience, and it comes from believing that the product can do what you say that the product will do. Confidence shows when you confidently expect the prospect to buy.

————————————

YOUR NOTES

Qualifying the Prospect

In the process of selling, there are several other steps that you must take before you close. The first step, of course, is qualifying. You cannot sell a product until you have thoroughly qualified the prospect. Every one of us has been in a situation where we have walked into a store or onto a used car lot, and somebody comes up and says, "Why don't you take it?" Or "Are you going to buy it today?" They try to close you without ever asking you what it is you want or what you need. They forget to qualify.

———————————

YOUR NOTES

Four Questions for Qualifying

To qualify effectively, you have to find the answers to four questions. Question number one; does the prospect need what you're selling? Question number two, can the prospect use what you're selling?

Many people may need a piece of high tech equipment, but they may not be able to use it because of the people or the structure of the organization. Number three; can the person afford the product? And number four; does the person want the product?

———————————————

YOUR NOTES

Desire Comes Before Closing

Before you can close, the prospect has to have demonstrated that he or she has a desire to enjoy the benefits of your product or service. Once you've given your presentation, qualified the prospect in all four of these categories and determined that he/she wants to buy it, you're in a position to begin closing. Much of the sale is made in the presentation. In some products, especially in real estate, the close is largely determined by how well you present the product to the prospect.

———————————————

YOUR NOTES

Why the Close Is Difficult

The moment of closing is always difficult. There is always a moment of tension. There is always a feeling of stress on the part of the prospect. This is a form of buyer's remorse, in advance. Whenever a prospect reaches a point where he has to make an important decision, whenever he has to spend money, tension wells up inside of him. He experiences the fear of failure.

Every one of us, as human beings, experiences this fear of failure. The tension in the closing moments of the sale is caused by the fear of making a mistake, the fear of buying the wrong thing, the fear of paying too much, the fear of being criticized by other people. What happens when a person feels this fear? It is very much like having a spear in the stomach. What do they do as a result?

———————————————

YOUR NOTES

They back away.

Whenever he experiences this fear, he retreats. He says things like, "let me think it over," or "can you leave me some material," or " could you call me back next week, I have to talk it over with someone else, I have to check it out first, I can't afford it," and so on. These are all different ways that the prospect tells you that, "I don't think if I make this decision it'll be the right thing for me."

——————————————

YOUR NOTES

The Fear of Rejection

The second major stumbling block at the close is the fear of rejection. It is the fear of the prospect saying "no." Each of us, deep down inside, has a fear of being told "no", a fear of being rejected. Because of this fear, we very cleverly organize our lives in such a way that we don't put ourselves in front of people that say "no."

And by the way, if you have a problem with the word "no," you've picked a very interesting profession to get into, because four out of five sales calls end with "no's," even in the very best of times. In the finest economy, with the finest product, 80 percent of the people you talk to are going to say no.

One of the key factors in successful selling is to be prepared to hear a no and continue. When the prospect says, "No I don't think so," you must be able to just let it roll off your back like water off a duck's back.

YOUR NOTES

Rejection Is Not Personal

You must realize that a no is not personal. It is not aimed at you as an individual. When a person says no to you, they're not saying no to you in most cases, they're saying no to your offering, for a series of reasons, most of which you can do nothing about. Your job is to face your fear, confront your fear, do the thing you fear, and ask for the order.

———————————

YOUR NOTES

Expect Sales Resistance

Sales resistance is normal and natural in every sales conversation. At the moment of making a buying decision, this fear, this uneasiness, this tension starts to build up. Your job is to get through that moment of tension as quickly and as painlessly as possible. That's what good closing techniques are for.

Just remember that closing techniques are not ways of manipulating other people. They are not techniques to get people to buy things they don't want, don't need, can't use, and can't afford. They are techniques to help get people past that moment of tension. The professional salesperson takes the prospect smoothly past the point of closing, making it easy for the prospect to buy. The unprofessional salesperson sits there wishing and hoping, and at the end of the presentation, he says, "Well, what do you think?"

Have you ever done that? "Well, what do you think?" And you know what the prospect says? His stress and tension starts to build. His heart starts pounding faster. His blood pressure increases. He feels the adrenaline pumping and the "fight or flight" reaction comes over him.

Finally he says, "Well, I think I'd like to think it over." Or "I think I have to talk it over with someone else." Even if he wants it, the tension is too great. This is why you must know how to ask a closing question. This tension on the part of the prospect that kills so many sales is why you must learn how to close smoothly and well.

This is why you must know a series of closing techniques.

———————————————

YOUR NOTES

Closing

1. Closing On Appointments

The first closing technique is aimed at getting appointments on the telephone. If you use a telephone to get appointments, you know how difficult and frustrating it can be. Many people do not use the telephone because they've been rejected and turned down so many times. The very thought of telephoning triggers feelings of anger and frustration. As a result, they seek every other way possible to make contacts. The telephone however is the finest and the fastest way to get good appointments, if you know how to use it properly.

In approaching the prospect by telephone, the first thing that you say has to be something that breaks preoccupation, grabs attention, and points to the result or benefit of the product. Here is an example. I used to sell sales training programs. I would qualify my prospects when I called to make appointments. I found that I could get appointments nine out of ten times with qualified prospects using this very simple technique.

I would call up and ask the receptionist, "Who is the person who makes the decisions regarding sales training in your company?" She would say, "that would be Mr. Jones." I would say, "thank you. What is his first name, please?" Bill Jones. I would ask, "Could I speak to Mr. Jones?"

I would then say, "Hello Mr. Jones, this is ______ __________. Would you like to see a method that would enable you to increase your sales by 20 to 30 percent over the next 12 months?"

If you're speaking to the right person, your opening question will be aimed at something that is relevant and important, and at something that the other person needs or wants. What do sales managers sit around and think about all day long? Increasing sales!

When you say, would you like to see a system that would enable you to increase your sales by 20 to 30 percent over the next 12 months, the first question that the prospect asks should be, "What is it?"

That is where you go into the close for the appointment. And when you are telephoning for an appointment, you are telephoning to sell an appointment, not to sell a product. The biggest mistake you can make is to start describing your product on the telephone. The prospect will almost always say, "Well, no, I'm sorry, I'm not interested, can't afford it, I don't have the time" and so on.

All you are selling is ten minutes of his time. When the prospect says, "What is it?" You respond by saying, "that's exactly what I want to talk to you about. I need about ten minutes of your time."

"I'll show you what I've got, and you can judge for yourself if it's what you want." If the prospect asks, "How much is it?" This is the way you handle it. You say, "Mr. Prospect, if it's not exactly what you're looking for, there's no charge at all." This is a very powerful response. Get the price issue out of the way immediately. "If it's not exactly what you're looking for, it doesn't cost you anything."

If the prospect then asks, "Well, could you tell me a little about it," I'd say, "Well, that's exactly why I need just ten minutes of your time. In ten minutes, I'll be able to show you what I've got, and you can judge for yourself if it's what you're looking for.

Remember that good prospects are always busy and hard to get to. Poor prospects are not busy, and they're easy to get to. If you call up somebody and you ask for an appointment, and they say, sure come on over anytime, you can be sure the person isn't going buy anything from you.

The prospect may say, "Well, could you tell me a little bit about it. " You say, "Yes, I would like to, but there's something I have to show you."

As soon as you say the word show, you've sidestepped the request to describe it on the telephone. If the prospect says, "Well, could you send me something in the mail?" I would say, "I would like to send it to you in the mail, but you know how bad the mails are. Why don't I drop it off personally some time this afternoon?"

If the prospect is at all interested, he will say, "Okay, drop it off personally sometime this afternoon." I would then ask, "Will you be there?" "Yes, I'll be there." I would say, "Okay, about 3:00, I'll be in your neighborhood. I'll drop it off personally."

Don't mail information. When people say, "Send me some information in the mail," what they're really saying is, "Go away. I'm not interested." When you send it to them in the mail, it usually goes right into the wastebasket. If you're going to send things in the mail, it is better that you put it in the envelope, throw it in your own wastebasket, and save yourself the cost of a stamp.

Sometimes, we make the mistake of thinking that when we mail information, we're actually making sales. But only sales are sales, not mailing out sales information that no one reads. You ask for ten minutes of his time, and this is the key expression, "You be the judge."

"You decide for yourself if this is what you're looking for." You repeat, "All I need is ten minutes of your time and you can judge for yourself." This assures him that you will only be there for a short period of time.

You assure him that you will put no pressure on him. You will just show them what you've got, like an Arab trader in the bazaar lays out his wares. If the prospect doesn't express some interest within ten minutes, you'll be going.

I have found that if you ask for 30 minutes, you will have to wait for weeks, maybe forever. If you ask for 10 minutes, you can almost always be slipped in. Don't make the mistake of using the old high-pressure salesman's trick of saying, "How about 10:00 today or 2:00 tomorrow?" This alternative close has been used so many times that it just insults the prospect.

Just say "Sometime this afternoon or maybe some time tomorrow?" Be very flexible. Sometimes the prospect says, "Why don't you call me on Monday, and we'll set up an appointment.?" What you say to him is this, "Look, I've got my calendar right here. Is your calendar handy?" Of course, the prospect is sitting at his desk, with his calendar handy. You say, "Let's set up a time right now; how about 10:00 Monday morning?

Don't allow yourself to be put off with this "Call me back on Monday." It is just another way of getting out of seeing you face to face. The very best customers you will ever have are the ones you're going to have to fight to see the first time. They are also the ones who buy the most. When they try to put you off, when they try to avoid you make excuses, what they're saying is that this may be a very good prospect. Somebody is going to get to that prospect, and sell that prospect, and it might as well be you.

Be persistent, be polite, and be firm. Say, "All I need is ten minutes of your time. Just ten minutes will be enough. Give me ten minutes and you'll be able to decide for yourself." Just sell ten minutes. If he asks you for details about your product or service, you say, "It's too involved to go into on the phone, but it'll just take ten minutes, and I'll show you what I've got." Sell only that ten-minute appointment. If you cannot close on telephone appointments, you can't even get to first base.

Resolve to become very good on the telephone. If you are tense about using the phone, if you're nervous, it's because you've had frustrating experiences in the past. You will become more confident as you become more competent.

———————————

YOUR NOTES

2. The Approach Close

The next close is called the approach close. You use this right at the beginning of the sales presentation.

The purpose of the approach close is to get the prospect to make a commitment to giving you a decision at the end of the presentation rather than him saying afterwards, "I have to think it over."

The approach close is a technique you use when you have a product or service which is used and needed by almost everybody. Recognize that sales resistance is the highest at the beginning of the sales presentation. This is because we live in a commercial society. Someone is trying to sell us something hundreds of times every day. We see, hear or are exposed to thousands of advertisements each day, in the form of radio, newspaper, television, billboard, buses, and so on. Everybody's trying to sell us something, so we have natural sales resistance, from the age of five years.

There is a simple and powerful way to overcome this natural resistance at the beginning of the sales conversation. You simply say this. "Mr. Prospect, I'm not here to sell you anything right now. All I'm going to do is to show you some of the reasons why people have bought this product, and continue to buy it over the years.

And all I ask you to do is look at the reasons why others have bought it and judge for yourself. You can then tell me, one way or another, whether or not these reasons apply to you and to your situation. Is that fair? I'll just show you why others have bought it and you just tell me whether it makes sense of not to you.

The person will usually agree to this proposal. What you're doing is offering him a deal. The deal is, "I won't try to sell you, if you'll listen with an open mind to my presentation."

The prospect usually, "Okay, I'll listen with an open mind." You then go through your normal presentation.

At the end of the presentation, the prospect cannot then say, "Well, I have to think it over."

You say, "Mr. Prospect, you promised you'd give me an answer one way or another."

It's a very simple close. "You promised you'd give me an answer one way or another. And from what you've said, it seems that this product is just ideal for your situation." You can then go right through to the close.

———————————

YOUR NOTES

3. The Demonstration Close

Another closing technique that you can use, right at the beginning, is called the demonstration close. It is very effective. You can use this close in almost any situation.

The demonstration close is what you use to qualify the prospect with your opening words, and to get a clear statement from the prospect that he is in a position to buy and to pay for this product. We used to use this close in selling mutual funds. We'd say, "Mr. Prospect, if I could show you the very best investment you've ever seen, are you in a position to put $5,000 into right now?"

The prospect might say, "Well, I don't know. I haven't got $5,000 right now." Could you invest four?" "Well, I don't know." "How about three?" "Well, yes, I could invest three thousand." "So, if I could show you the best investment you've ever seen, you could put $3,000 into it?"

What you've done now is that you have changed the focus of the discussion. The discussion is no longer about whether or not the prospect listens to your presentation. The focus of the discussion is, "Can you demonstrate or prove that you actually have an investment or a product that is as good as you say?"

Another thing you can say is, "If I can show you the best sales training system that you've seen, are you in a position to commit yourself to it right now?" The prospect says, "Well, if it's that good, I could make a decision right now." You then you go through your presentation. At the end of the presentation, the prospect can't say, "Well, I have to check with the boss. I have to talk to Harry. I have to check our budget." He has told you, in advance, that he can make the decision.

He has already said, "Yes I have the money. Yes I'm qualified. Yes, I'm in a position to make a decision." So, a good strong opening question that grabs attention and offers to give the prospect exactly what he wants, is very powerful. If your question is well phrased, the only questions he should ask is, " What is it?" He should say, "Tell me more about it."

"If I could show you exactly what you're looking for, are you in a position to make a decision today?" In real estate, for example, I've seen this close used over and over again. One of the first questions that you should ask people when you take them out is, "If we could find the exact house you're looking for, when would you want to take possession?" Ask them as you get into the car.

They may tell you they don't know. They may tell you that they're not in the market at all. They are just taking up your time looking at houses because they have some spare time.

This not an invasive question. It's not a rude question. Your time is valuable and you are entitled to ask if this prospect is really capable of buying.

YOUR NOTES

4. The Hot Button Close

The hot button close is considered by many sales professionals to be the most powerful closing technique of all. The hot button close is based on the fact that 80 percent of the buying decision is determined by 20 percent of the product features and benefits.

In my experience, probably 90 percent of the buying decision is determined by about 10 percent of the product features. It is up to you to find the hot button, the key benefit of your offering that is what the prospect wants more than anything else. You then to push this hot button over and over again. Every time you mention the hot button, the prospect's desire to own your product or service goes up. Every time you talk about something that is not really important to him, his desire to purchase it goes down.

Good sales people are those who question skill fully and listen carefully to the answers. They listen for what is called the Freudian slip. The Freudian slip concept says that if you ask enough questions and give prospects enough opportunity to talk, they will tell you everything that you need to know to sell them.

That's why the old saying, "Telling is not selling" is true. You are only really selling when you are asking questions and giving them the opportunity to tell you what they're looking for, what they want, what they need, what they're concerned about, what their worries are. You are only really selling when you are listening attentively.

The more you ask questions and listen, the more likely it is that the prospect will say, "This is what I'm looking for." This is the key benefit. There's a key benefit for every product or service that a prospect must be assured of receiving he can buy. Until he hears or sees that key benefit, he won't make the buying decision.

One of my favorite stories is about a real estate agent who takes a couple to see a home for sale. It's an old house. It's what they call a starter home, a pre-owned starter home, one that requires lots of work, a handyman's special.

They pull up to the house. In the back yard, there is a beautiful flowering cherry tree. And the salesman asks the couple, "What do you think of this house?" The wife says, "Harry, look at that beautiful flowering cherry tree. Ever since I was a girl, I wanted to have a house with a beautiful flowering cherry tree in the back yard." And Harry says, "Shut up." You know how Harry is. He always says, "Shut up." They get out of the car and go into the house. The salesman is no dummy. He walks in behind them. Harry, Mr. Tough Guy, comes in and immediately says, "Look at this, you will have to replace the steps."

The salesman says, "Yes, but look at that beautiful flowering cherry tree out in the yard." They walk into the house and Harry says, "This carpet is worn out; it will have to be replaced."" Yes," the salesman says, "But from here, you can see that beautiful flowering cherry tree, Mrs. Smith." As they walk through the house, they say, "Look at this living room. They will have to put in new baseboards and new lights." "Yes, but look at the beautiful view you have of that lovely flowering tree from this room." This happens with almost every room they go into. "The kitchen needs new plumbing" "Yes but you can see that beautiful flowering cherry tree out the window."

"The bedrooms are too small." "But look at the view of that beautiful flowering cherry tree." At the end of the presentation, Mrs. Smith, who makes the buying decision in every home purchase, says Harry, I sure do love that beautiful flowering cherry tree. This was the hot button. And they eventually bought the house because of that flowering cherry tree.

Your job is to discover and then push the hot button over and over again. What amazes me is that sales people will go out and talk, talk, talk, but will not ask enough questions to find out the prospect's hot button.

The prospect will say, "I'm really interested in a house with a pool."

The salesperson will say, "Isn't this a beautiful yard?" "Yes, but it doesn't have a pool in it." "Here's a beautiful house; you could put a tennis court over there." "Yes, but it doesn't have a pool." "This house has a wonderful basement." "Yes, but it doesn't have a pool." The prospect keeps saying, "What I want is a pool." As a professional, you listen for that hot button, and you build your selling efforts around that. Until you know the hot button, it is almost impossible for you to make the sale.

—————————————

YOUR NOTES

5. The Trial Close

The trial close is a technique that a professional sales person asks throughout the presentation to find out how well he is doing.

It is also called the check close. You use it to check your progress. You present a part of your product or service offering and then you ask, "What do you think of this so far? Does this make sense to you? Is this what you're looking for? Is this what you had in mind? Is this an improvement on what you are doing right now?"

These are all trial closes. The best thing about a trial close is that the prospect can answer "no" and it doesn't end the presentation.

For example, you could ask, "Is this the sort of layout that you're looking for?" The prospect might say, "No." You can then say, "That's good to know; we have several other layouts." You could ask, "Do you like this color?" If the prospect says, "Yes," you know you are getting closer to a sale. If the prospect says, "No, I don't like that color," you can say, "That's alright; we have several other colors available."

The trial or check close is like a signpost at a crossroads that tells you which way to go. Imagine that you are traveling down a road and you come to a fork, and at the fork, you say, "How do you like this. Are we on the right road?" At the next fork, you check again to make sure that the customer is still happy with what you are showing him or her.

Good sales people ask check closes throughout the sales conversation. They never present a piece of information without confirming that they are on the right track with a check close. For example, you drive up to the front of the house. You then ask, "How do you like the outside look of this house?" You come in the door and you ask, "What do you think about this entry hallway?" "Do you like this color scheme?" Yes or no? "Do you like the way this is laid out?" Yes or no? Professional salespeople ask questions continually, and the answers give them steady feedback that enables them eventually to develop a clear picture of exactly what the prospect wants.

YOUR NOTES

6. The Power of Suggestion Close

The power of suggestion close is based on the fact that we are all very susceptible to the suggestive influences of people around us. For example, when a person becomes excited about something, that excitement is contagious. Other people can become excited as well. When a person becomes enthusiastic about something, that enthusiasm can be contagious, as well.

The way you use the power of suggestion close is by creating emotions in the prospect with words or pictures. For example, you can say, "You're really going to enjoy the way this car handles on the road. My brother has one of these cars and he just loves the way it grips the road when he corners!"

In other words, you talk to the prospect as if he already owns the product or service you are selling. You say, " You are really going to be happy when you travel in this car this summer." "You are really going to enjoy this holiday to Europe." "You are going to love this tour." "You are going to enjoy living in this neighborhood. This is one of the best neighborhoods in this part of the city."

You talk to them throughout as if they had already made the decision to buy. You continually create mental pictures of what it's going to be like to use, to enjoy, to benefit, and to own the product.

As you these emotional work pictures, their thinking changes. Instead of thinking, "Should I buy it or not?" they are thinking of how they're going to enjoy it once they own it. You should always be positively and confidently talking to your prospects in language that suggests that they already own your product or service. This language exerts a powerful influence on their thinking and decision-making.

YOUR NOTES

7. The Invitational Close

The invitational close is used when you simply invite the prospect to make a buying decision. My favorite invitational close is, "Why don't you give it a try?" Why don't you give it a try? When you say, "why don't you give it a try?" you are saying or suggesting that making the purchase decision is no big deal. It is sort of something that you can try. Like saying, why don't you give the car a try? It is an easy decision to make.

For example, why don't you give that car a try? You are suggesting that, if you don't like it, you can try something else. "Why don't you give it a try?" is a very subtle way of saying that you still have your options open.

Another version of the invitational close is "Why don't you take it? " A real estate salesman found that his sales increased almost 40% using this technique. Each time he showed a house to a couple, he would ask a trial closing question like, "How do you like the house?" If they said, "It seems very nice," he would then ask, "Why don't you buy it? Why don't you make an offer?"

It is amazing how many prospects will say, "Well, sure. Why not?"

Another invitational close is simply, "How many would you like? Or, what color would you like?

Or, would you like us to get started on this right way? Or, is this what you had in mind?" In other words, you invite the prospect to make a decision. You don't come to the end of the presentation and then ask, "Well, what do you think?"

There is the story of the sales person who comes back to the office and says, "Boy, did I have a lot of good interviews today." The other salesperson says, "Yeah, I didn't sell anything either." Remember that you do not offend people by asking them to make a buying decision once they have indicated an interest in owning or enjoying, the benefits of your product or service. Don't be afraid to ask, to invite them to buy.

YOUR NOTES

8. The Just Suppose Close

You use the just suppose close when the prospect says that he can't afford what you are selling. You reply and say, "Mr. Prospect, just suppose that price is not an obstacle and that we can deal with your price concerns to your complete satisfaction. Can we do that just for just a moment so that I can finish my presentation?" The prospect will usually say, "Okay." By the time you get to the end of the presentation, you should have explained the value of what it is you are selling in such detail, that when you tell him the price, he will see that it makes sense.

When you mention the price, and they say, "Wow, that's a lot of money, what they are really saying is this: "You haven't given me enough reasons to justify that price." Remember that a price objection is really a price question. A price question is when he says, "That's too expensive." What he is asking is, "From what you've told me so far, I don't see how you can charge so much for your product or service. Can you give me some more information?"

Remember that it is not the price but the reasons for the price that are most important. You say, "Mr. Prospect, it may sound like a lot of money, but let me tell you why it costs what it does, and why it is worth every penny." You then explain the value of your product that more than justifies the amount you charge for it.

Be proud of your prices. When the prospect says things like, "It costs too much." Or, "You charge more than your competition." You say, "Mr. Prospect, you're right. As a matter of fact, it costs $1,227 more than our closest competition."

"And yet we sell thousands of these every year to very intelligent people like yourself. Would you like to know why?" You then go on to explain why people buy from you, and continue to buy, even at higher prices.

You have to get price out of the way at the beginning. Other than that, it just sits there like a big orang-utan in the middle of the path between you and the sales.

——————————————

YOUR NOTES

9. The Sudden Death Close

The sudden death close is a technique you use as an ultimatum. You have had an experience where you've made a presentation to a person or to a company, and they've looked at it, and not made a decision. You have gone back to see them and they say they have to think about it a little bit more. You go back again, and they tell you that they still have to think about it a bit longer. They won't give you an answer, yes or no.

After four or five visits, you find that you're spending too much time going back to this person who won't make a decision. It is time for the sudden death close, which works successfully about 50 percent of the time. Here's how you use it: You fill out the entire sales contract with all details, except for the signature, exactly the way you've discussed the product or service up to now. You then take it back to the prospect and you say, "Mr. Prospect, we've discussed this quite a bit now, and I know this is taking up a lot of your time. It's taking up a lot of my time, as well. And either this is a good idea for you or it's not. So, one way or another, let's make a decision right now. What do you say?"

You then take out the contract, put your pen on top of it, slide it across the desk, and say, "If you'll just authorize this, we can get started right away." You then sit in complete silence. Remember, after every closing technique, the key is to shut up. The key to the effectiveness of this technique is to be perfectly silent, and wait. Sometimes, the silence can go on for several minutes, or even longer.

But the longer you wait quietly, without speaking, the more likely it is that the prospect will decide to buy. The greater the tension, the more likely the sale. The only pressure that you are allowed to use in a sales presentation is the pressure of the silence after you've asked the closing question. And the basic rule is this, "He who speaks first, or she who speaks first, after the closing question, loses."

The best time to close a sale is at the end of your presentation, not the next day or "come back next week" or "let me think about it." The prospect has more information and is closer to making a decision at the end of the sales presentation than at any other time.

———————————

YOUR NOTES

10. The Sharp Angle Close

You use the sharp angle close when the prospect wants the product and is bringing up all sorts of what we call smoke screen objections. These are not serious reasons for not buying. They are just excuses for not going ahead with the sale. For example, they say, "Well, I don't know if we can afford the monthly payments."

With the sharp angle, or bear trap close, you turn the objection around and use it as a reason for buying. You say, "If we could spread the payments over a longer period and get them down, would you take it?"

You use the objection as a way of closing by answering it with a solution and then asking for the order.

You close on the objection.

The prospect says, "I don't think that your product will perform to my specifications." You say, "If we can prove to you that it will, would you take it?" The prospect says, "Well, I don't think you can get it here on time." You immediately say, "If we can get it to you on schedule, would you take it?"

This approach forces the prospect to say either, "Yes, I'll take it," or "That's not the real reason why

I'm not making a buying decision." This gives you a chance to uncover exactly why the prospect is hesitating.

YOUR NOTES

11. The Instant Reverse Close

The instant reverse close is a technique you can use all the time. It takes little bit of courage to use the first time, but it is very effective. Let us say that a prospect says, "I can't afford it."

You immediately respond by saying, "That's exactly why you should buy it.!" The prospect will react with surprise. " What? How do you mean?" You then say, "That's exactly why you should take it, Mr. Prospect." And then you explain how and why he will benefit from paying more than he was expecting to for what you are selling. You may not even have an answer when you say this, so you have to think of the answer very quickly. The answer just has to be logical. It doesn't have to be great. It just has to be logical.

Here is another way you can use the instant reverse close. You call a prospect to arrange an appointment and the person on the line says, "I'm not interested." (Have you ever heard that before?) You say, "Mr. Prospect, that's why exactly why I'm calling." The prospect will be caught off guard. " What?" You say, "Mr. Prospect, most of our very best customers were not interested when we first contacted them. But now they've become our best customers and they recommend us to their friends."

The prospect will usually say, "Really, what is it then?" And you say, "That's exactly what I would like to show you, and I just need ten minutes of your time." And immediately, you move on to close on the appointment.

A prospect says, "We don't use that in our house." You say, "That's exactly why you should take it." Why? "Well, if you keep using the same product, Mr. Prospect, you'll never have any idea that the, of the better products that are available on the market." And then you proceed to ask for a few minutes to show the prospect how your product or service is better or more affordable than they might have thought.

———————————————

YOUR NOTES

12. The Change Places Close

The change places close is very simple. You are giving a presentation and the prospect will not tell you the key issue, the number one reason why they won't buy. As you know, for every product or service that a person can buy, there is a key benefit that they want and there's a key issue or a key objection that is stopping them from buying it. And until you can find out what that key objection is and deal with it, they will never buy from you. Many of your closing techniques are ways of getting the person to tell you what is stopping them from making a decision.

Here is how you use the change places close in this situation. You say, "Mr. Prospect, would you change places with me just for a second?"

"Please put yourself in my shoes," (which prospects will do if they are at all empathetic.) You say, "Imagine if you were talking to somebody that you really respected, and you were showing them a product or a service that was really good for them, and they wouldn't tell you why it is they wouldn't make a decision, one way or another. What would you do if you were in my position?"

Almost invariably the prospect will say, "Well, I'll tell you why I'm hesitating." And he will give you the reasons why he is hesitating, enabling you to answer them and go on with the sale. You can simply ask, "Mr. Prospect, what would you do in if you were in my position?"

To prompt him to give you more information, you can say, "Tell me, is it the money?" If it's not the money, he will say, no it's not the money. You can then ask, "Then may I ask what it is that is causing you to hesitate?" He may say, "Yes, it's the money." You can then say, "Mr. Prospect, what would we have to do to satisfy you on that point?" Or, "What would we have to do to do a deal today?" Or, "How far apart are we?" These are powerful closing questions.

Sometimes you will find that you are very close on the price. You may find that it is another issue. Sometimes people say that they will not pay over X number of dollars because their brother-in-law got one just like it for X number of dollars. And you could find yourself just a few dollars apart. So ask them, how far apart are we? Or, Mr. Prospect, what do we have to do to do a deal today? You tell me and I'll find out if it's possible.

Most people are honest. He will say, this is what we would have to do to do a deal. And you say, "Okay, let me see what I can do." And at least you're still in the game. You're still in the ring. You still have a chance to sell.

——————————————

YOUR NOTES

13. The Secondary Close

This is one of the most popular closing techniques of all time. You use it to close on a minor point. Sometimes it is called the minor question close. For example, imagine you are selling a car, and you say, "By the way, will you want the cassette or CD player with the stereo sound surround system?"

It doesn't really matter to you which he chooses. In either case, he has decided to buy the car. Let us say you are selling a house. You ask, "By the way, would you want to take possession on the 1st or the 15th of the month? Whichever date they select, they've made the decision to buy the house. In other words, you close on a minor question rather on the entire purchase decision. It is much easier for a prospect to make a decision on a minor point than on the whole offer.

You can always find a minor point to close on. You can say, "Will that be cash or charge?" Even before the prospect has decided whether she wants to buy. "Well, I'll pay cash." They've made the buying decision. How they pay for it is a minor issue.

YOUR NOTES

14. The Alternative Close

The alternative close is based on this rule. Never offer a prospect the choice between something and nothing. Always make it a choice between one of two items. Always offer him a choice between Product A or Product B. " Which house do you like best? This one or this one? Which car do you prefer? The 2-door or the 4-door? Which type of tires do you want? The radial or the standard?" Always give them at least two choices. The prospect will answer you and say, "Well, I like product A better or I like product B better, or I don't like either product." You can then ask why. This gives you an opportunity to continue selling. But don't ever ask, "Do you want this or not?"

————————————

YOUR NOTES

15. The Preference Close

Always ask, "Which do you prefer? " This is called the preference close. Which do you prefer? Asking people which they prefer is a good way of finding out where you are in the sales presentation. This is another version of the Alternative Close and it is very helpful in getting a buying response from a prospect.

YOUR NOTES

16. The Assumption Close

The assumption close is often called the "talking past the sale" close. You simply assume that the person has decided to buy. You talk exactly as if he has just said, "Yes, I'll take it." You assume the sale and ask something like, "How would you like to make payment?" or "Where would you want this delivered?" or "How soon do you need it?"

For example, imagine that you have just finished your presentation. You ask, "Well, who is going to handle the mortgage arrangements for this?" Even before the prospect says, "Yes, I'll take it," you ask, "Who will handle the mortgage arrangements?" You assume that he has decided to buy. You talk past the sale and you go on to wrap up the details. This assumption close is one of the most powerful closes you can learn. It only takes a little practice to master.

———————————

YOUR NOTES

17. The Take Away Close

With the take away close, even before the prospect says yes or no, you begin to suggest that the product may not be available. You might be out of stock. Sometimes people are not even aware that they want the item until you suggest that they may not be able to get it.

One example of the take away close is the situation where you finish the sales presentation and the prospect has not yet made a decision. You have answered all their objections. He starts saying something like, "Well, it seems kind of expensive. I don't know if we can afford it right now."

You say, "Excuse me for a moment. We were talking about the blue one, weren't we? We've really had a run on the blue ones lately. They are very popular. Let me call the office (or the warehouse), and make sure we still have them in stock. May I use your telephone?"

The prospect suddenly becomes aware that he might not be able to get it. He says, "Yes. You can use my telephone." At that moment, he has made the decision to buy. You can phone, confirm availability, and then hang up and say, "You're in luck. There's only one left and I reserved it for you.'

Many people don't realize how badly they want something until you suggest to them that they can't have it. When we are teenagers, we call this "playing hard to get." You didn't even know that you were interested in that boy or girl until he or she began playing this game with you.

They use technique in stores all the time. You are looking at an item and the salesperson says, "Do you like that?" You say, "Yes, it looks all right." The salesperson immediately says, "Well, let me make sure we have it in your size. I'll go and check." You say, "Yes, make sure you have it in my size." You have just decided to buy it.

The salesperson returns and says, "Yes we do have it in your size, just one." And suddenly you want it, before someone else gets it. This is a closing technique they use in ladies' boutiques. They all use it.

Here is another example you are familiar with; a woman is trying on something in a store. It's expensive. (This technique is never used with anything cheap.) When someone is trying on something that's expensive, the sales clerks have an invisible signal. They wave their hands or ring a bell, or something. It causes all the other sales clerks to come running over. You're trying on something that is ridiculously expensive. And they all rush up and say, "Ooh, that looks very good on you, doesn't it?" All the sales clerks cluster around like hens. They cluck and they say, "Yes, that looks really good on you. Oh, that looks good on you." And you say, "Really? You really think so?" And they say, "Oh, yes, yes, yes!"

As soon you say, "Well, okay," they break up and all rush back to their customers. Meanwhile, you've bought the item.

My wife has come home with the funniest looking outfits as a result of being closed like this. But she wants to try it on for me because she's not quite sure if she made the right choice. She's not quite sure why she bought it at all. She comes in and she says, "Be perfectly honest with me." And I'll say, "I don't really think it suits you." And she will say, 'But everybody in the store said it looked great on me. And there was only one left in my size." Be very alert to this technique being used on you, or on someone you know.

———————————

YOUR NOTES

18. The Puppy Dog Close

This is one of the most powerful and best closes of all. It is based on the old story where the kids corner the parents and say, "We want a puppy. We want a puppy. We want a puppy." The parents, knowing what is involved in caring for a dog, say, "No! You're not getting a dog. You won't take proper care of it." The children then say, "Well, please just take us to the pet store and let us look at the puppies. Eventually the parents give in and take them to the store, but just to look.

The pet store owners are smart. They know what's going what the parent is thinking. They will then say, "You don't have to make a decision like this right away. You want to be sure. Why don't you take this little puppy home and just play with it for the weekend. And if you don't like it, you can bring it back on Monday." The kids say, "Yes, yes, yes, just for the weekend, just for the weekend!" And the parents say, "Well, all right. Just for the weekend. Just for Sunday." Well, by Sunday night, the kids have lost interest in the dog and the parents have fallen in love with it. As a result, they end up keeping the puppy, and the sale is made.

This method really works. Any time you can give your prospect an opportunity to touch, taste, feel, smell, or use the product, this is

a puppy dog close. One of the most successful photocopier distribution companies I've ever seen has one simple marketing and sales strategy. "Place machines." They have ten trucks and 30 sales people. All the salespeople do is to visit prospective customers and invite them to try out their machines at no charge for a week.

Once the prospect has used the machine for a week, he/she gets used to it. They like it. They enjoy its superior features to what they've been using in the past.

Initially they may say, "No, thank you. I'm not interested. I can't afford it." But after they have used it for a week, they become accustomed to it, enjoy the convenience of it, and they decide to keep it.

I used to have a friend who sold motor homes, big, expensive motor homes. They cost fifty thousand dollars and more. And in good times and bad, this salesman is one of the top motor home sales people in America.

Here is how he used the puppy dog close. A prospect would come in to look at a motor home. Now, this salesman knows that people who buy motor homes shop around before buying. They go to every single vendor of motor homes within one hundred miles. Motor home owners and purchasers are fanatics. And they know everything there is to know about motor homes. So when they come in, he meets with them and talks to them. He shows them through the motor homes. He doesn't try to close them. He establishes rapport with them. He tells them his name and he learns their names.

He gives them his business card. He gets their address and phone number. He says, "We have a newsletter on motor homes and we'll put you on the mailing list." The next weekend, he phones them at about ten or eleven o'clock Saturday morning. Now, where are most people at ten o'clock, eleven o'clock Saturday morning? They're at home. He says, "I'd like to take you out for lunch. I'd like to show you something absolutely fantastic. I'll pick you up at your home at 12:00."

They are pleasantly surprised and they agree. At 12:00 noon, he drives up in front of their home in a big, beautiful, $50,000 motor home. He invites them to get in and he tells them he has something neat to show them. Of course, they're a little curious. He then drives them to a beautiful park just outside the city that he lives in. The park has long, sloping hills and a lake. There are ducks and geese swimming in the lake. There are trees on the other side, and there are mountains in the distance.

He pulls up in this big motor home, swings a loop and stops so that you can sit at the kitchen table in the motor home, looking out the window at this beautiful view. He then says, "Sit down over here please." Once they are seated, he opens up the microwave, heats up the food, takes wine out of the refrigerator, puts it in a wine bucket, pours a glass for each of them, and then lays out the food, the china and the utensils. He sits down with them and he says, as they're eating, "Now, isn't this exactly what you want? Isn't this nice? Wouldn't it be nice to be able to do this every single weekend?"

He then says, "We have a special on a unit just like this. You can be driving it away by tomorrow afternoon. Then you will be set for the entire summer. What do you say?"

With this version of the puppy dog close, he sells more motor homes than almost anyone else in his industry. This method of selling gives people the chance to experience the product. And once they have tried it out and enjoyed the benefits, they buy it.

———————————————

YOUR NOTES

19. The Ben Franklin Close

The Ben Franklin close is one of the most powerful of all closing techniques for a very simple reason. This method closely parallels the way you and I think and make decisions in every area of our lives. We weigh the pros and cons. We look at the reasons in favor of a decision, and compare them with the reasons against making the decision.

The Ben Franklin originates with Benjamin Franklin, America's first self-mad millionaire. He developed the habit of making his decisions by taking a piece of paper and drawing a line down the center. He would write all the reasons in favor of making the decision on one side of the paper, and all the reasons opposed to the decision on the other side. He would then study the lists, and make his decision.

Whenever you are selling anything complex, this is an excellent method to use. When a prospect is having difficulty making up his mind because of a variety of different factors, you say, "Mr. Prospect, let's use the Ben Franklin decision making method. It's very simple. Ben Franklin used to use this and he became one of the richest men in America, making decisions on this basis. This is how it works. Take a piece of paper and draw a line down the center. Now, let's write down all the reasons in favor of making this purchase decision on the left hand side."

You then start listing off all the benefits and advantages of your product or service. " Remember we talked about this? And remember we talked about that? And we talked about this, and it does this, and it does that. And you have this and it includes this, and so on." You have the prospect write down every single buying reason you can think of. You restate all the good reasons for buying you product. And then you ask, "Is that everything, Mr. Prospect?"

"Can you think of anything else?" The prospect will eventually say, "No, I think that's everything." You then say, "Okay. Now, you fill out the other side." And you hand him the pad of paper and the pen.

You then sit quietly. Now, the sharpest prospect I've ever seen couldn't think of more than two or three reasons not to buy. You then look at his list and you say, "Well, Mr. Prospect, it looks like you've made your decision." The prospect will almost invariably say, "Well, yes. I guess I have." You can then go on to wrap up the sale.

I taught this close recently to a gentleman who sells and leases commercial real estate. He told me later that he had heard about this close all his life but he had never used it. Then he found himself in a negotiation with a large financial institution involving the sale of a series of properties between two institutions. He had been going back and forth with these people for three weeks. He said, finally, "Why don't we use the Benjamin Franklin decision making method?" Since they had nothing to lose, they decided to give it a try.

The vice president of the financial institution sat down and went through the Ben Franklin decision-making method. The salesperson told me that he followed the course, word for word from. After listing all the reasons in favor of proceeding, he turned it over to the vice president and said, "Now, you write the reasons opposed." The vice president could only come up with two or three reasons. The salesman then said, "Well, it looks like you've made your decision." The vice president said, "You're right. I have. Let's go with it." The salesman made about $50,000 commission on that sale. He said he was just amazed.

———————————

YOUR NOTES

20. The Summary Close

The summary close is use at the end of the presentation. You say, "Now, let's just briefly go over what we've talked about." You then summarize everything that you have just discussed and explained.

You summarize the features and the benefits, one by one. You go through the entire list, right down to the last reason he/she should buy. You ask, "Can you think of anything else?" The prospect will usually say "No." You then say, "Well, why don't you give it a try?" Or "Should we get started on this right away?"

Or "Is this what you had in mind?" Or "Why don't you take it?" And you just simply close the sale.

When you summarize all the reasons for buying the product or service one after another, you will bring the prospect to the point of his greatest buying desire for what you are selling.

For example, let's say that you're selling a home. You say, "Before you make a decision, let's look at all the features of this particular home. Well, it has this open kitchen. And it has a big backyard. And it has four bedrooms and a den. It has a double garage. It is on a quiet street, close to schools and shopping. It is well built and cared for. The price fits within your guidelines. And so on. You can probably get to forty positive features with a little bit of creativity.

The prospect says, "Wow! You're right. It's got all those features that we are looking for." They didn't realize how good the home was until it was perfectly described. A summary close can be a powerful way to convince the prospect overwhelmingly that what you are selling is a good deal.

———————————————

YOUR NOTES

21. The Order Sheet Close

The order sheet close is first used when the presentation begins. The prospect comes to see you, or you go to see him/ her, and the first thing you do is to pull out an order sheet and write the date on it. From then on, whenever the prospect says anything about the product or service, you write it on the order sheet. The prospect may try to stop you by saying, "Wait a minute, don't write anything down, I'm not buying anything today, I'm just looking."

You reply, "I understand, but I have a terrible memory for detail. So I like to write everything down. And if you don't buy anything today, we'll just throw it away. Okay?" And you just keep writing on the order sheet. Eventually the prospect gets used to seeing their information written on your sales contract. It becomes harder and harder not to buy when the sales conversation is over.

Another way that you can use the order sheet close is to just pull out the order sheet and start filling it out at the end of the presentation. Assume the sale and begin completing the details. The customer has to stop you from writing to stop the sale from proceeding.

Then you say, could you give me the exact spelling of your last name for mailing purposes.

They give you the exact smelling of their last name, they've made the decision to buy.

———————————————

YOUR NOTES

22. The Relevant Story Close

This is a powerful closing technique because we make all of our decisions with the right brain. And the right brain is stimulated by stories and pictures. Whenever you can create a picture, as in the power of suggestion close, or when you can use visual sales aids, or whenever you can tell a story about your product or service, you can stimulate the prospect to buy. People will remember a story about a product or service for years, but they will forget all the technical details in ten minutes.

You can use a relevant story close is when the prospect is having difficulty making a decision. You can use it in the middle of a presentation, as well. You can tell a relevant story about another prospect who

was hesitating about buying this product or service, and they finally decided to do it. Explain how happy they are today that they bought it.

23. The Door Knob Close

The door knob close is the close that you use when you have almost lost the sale. You've made your presentation. You've given it your best shot. The prospect has resisted. The prospect still has that one major issue, that one major objection. They're not telling you, because they know if they tell you, you're going to answer it and make the sale.

You have said everything you can think of. "Is it the money that you're concerned about. How far apart are we? What do we have to do to make a deal today?" The prospect keeps saying, "No. I'm not sure. I want to think it over." But he won't tell you what it is that's stopping him from buying. You know that he can afford it, and that he likes it, and wants it, and so on. Finally you say, "Mr. Prospect, thank you very much for your time. I know how busy you are, and I appreciate your talking to me. I'll be on my way now."

You close your briefcase, get to your feet and go to the door. As you get to the door, you put your hand on the door knob. At this moment, the prospect begins immediately to think about what he is going to do as soon as you leave. His sales resistance drops. You then turn around and say, "Oh, by the way, just before I go, I was wondering about something. I know that you're not going to buy anything today, but I wonder if you could help me with my sales presentation. Could you tell me, what was the real reason that you didn't buy today?"

Often the prospect will say, "Well, I'll tell you. The real reason was this." At that point, you take your hand off the door knob and you go back in. You set down your briefcase. You say,

"Mr. Prospect, I am so glad you told me that. That's my fault. Obviously I didn't explain that part of our offering to you. May I go over that point just one more time?"

Now you have the key reason for not buying. If you can answer it effectively, you can close 50 percent and more of these lost sales.

YOUR NOTES

24. The Referral Close

The basic rule is this. You should never leave a prospect or a purchaser without at least two referrals. When you've finished speaking to a prospect or a client, whether he buys of not, there are a variety of ways to get referrals. For example, you can say, "Mr. Prospect, I know you're not in a position to make a decision today. But could you give me the names of two or three people who you think may be able to take advantage of this offer?"

Now, this is a form of the alternative close. Give him a choice

between two or three referrals. The prospect will almost always pick two because it's easier. He will say, "Well, yes, I can give you a couple of names." And he'll give you the names. The prospect will always give you the first names that pop into his mind, people that he knows the best. These will be the names

of people that he is very familiar with, people that he works with or associates with.

You then say, "Mr. Prospect, would you happen to have their phone numbers handy?" They will usually have the phone numbers nearby. Now you've closed on the phone numbers. Then you ask, "Which of these prospects should I call first?" You are using another alternative close. He will probably say, "Well, call Bill first." Now he has answered affirmatively to four questions in a row. You then ask, "Mr. Prospect, would you call Bill right now and tell him that I'm coming over?"

By this time the prospect will say, "Well, sure." He will pick up the phone, call Bill and then send you over to see Bill, or whoever it happens to be. The reason why a referral is so much more powerful than a cold call is that with a referral, you have all the credibility of the person who is referring you. With a cold call, you go in with no credibility at all. And credibility, the amount that the prospect believes you, is the critical factor in buying.

You need 100 percent credibility before the prospect will buy. If you get a referral, you start off with 90 percent credibility. If somebody that you know and respect sends somebody to see you, you'll give that person the same treatment, the same courtesy that you would give to your friend. Always ask for referrals and never leave a presentation, if you possibly can, without at least two referrals.

Here is another idea with regard to referrals. Go back to all of your previous customers, call them up and ask them how they are doing. Are they happy with what they bought? Do they have any problems or questions? Is there anything that you can do for them? And, and if possible, go and call on them personally.

I have a friend who's an excellent sales person. Every January, right after the holidays, he goes and calls on every single customer he's got. He spends two or three weeks calling on back on his the people who have already bought from him.

After making sure that they don't have any problems, making sure they're happy, he gets two or three referrals from each. It takes him six months to work through those referrals. He makes half his sales for the year without any cold calling. Any person who's been in selling for more than 90 days should be working off of referrals almost 100 percent of the time. Referrals that people give you, or referrals that come to you as a result of good things that you've done in the marketplace are worth their weight in gold.

———————————————

YOUR NOTES

The sixteen closing keys

Now, here are the 16 time-tested closing keys you and your sales force can use immediately. They work for both products and services, big ticket or small. These keys can be adjusted to your personality, your products, and your prospects. Here are 16 closing keys to clinch any sale:

1. The Beyond Any Doubt Close. You close by assuming the prospect's going to buy. Take it for granted the answer is yes. You are 100 percent certain — you can imagine no other outcome. You sweep the buyer forward with this positive assumption, beyond any doubt.

——————————————

YOUR NOTES

2. The Little Question Close. By getting the buyer to decide something of secondary importance, like upholstery color in an automobile, you make the prospect tell you he or she is ready to buy. ("Will that be cash or charge?" "Shall I ship it by UPS or FedX?") That's the little question.

YOUR NOTES

3. The Do Something Close. Nine sales in ten should be closed by physical action. ("Just OK this slip and I'll call the plant right now.")

Action is the easiest, surest, quickest way. It implies consent. Just do something.

——————————————

YOUR NOTES

4. The Coming Event Close. You announce an impending event to hasten the decision. ("Prices are going up next month. Initial this form now!") When you suggest the possibility of loss, the buyer is putty in your hands.

———————————————

YOUR NOTES

5. The Third Party Endorsement Close. You tell stories about, or get referrals from, happy customers. ("Don't take my word for it." "Listen to what happened to Joe Weaver!") It's not what you say, it's what they say — the third party.

YOUR NOTES

6. The Something for Nothing Close. You end your presentation with a special bonus — appealing to that something- for-nothing hot button in each human being. Many buyers, seeing themselves as the center of the universe, will not sign unless they're getting something special. This can be, and usually is, a trivial thing. But it often locks up the sale — something for nothing.

——————————————

YOUR NOTES

7. The Ask and Get Close. At times, the best strategy is asking boldly for the order. Use this carefully, at the right time, under the right conditions. Many people are just waiting to be asked! One sure thing: You don't ask, and you don't get.

—————————————

YOUR NOTES

8. The Choice Close. Don't ask if, ask which. ("Which color do you prefer?" "Which do you like — 30-day or 90-day terms?") Give your buyer a choice where you win either way.

———————————————

YOUR NOTES

9. The Appeal to Pride Close. Paint a vivid picture. ("Imagine how you'll feel driving up in this family van!") Pride is powerful.

———————————

YOUR NOTES

10. The Future Dating Close. Your prospect is really not ready to buy now? Pin down delivery three months, or even a year, ahead. Better than letting a competitor walk away with it. That's future dating.

———————————————

YOUR NOTES

11. The Colombo Close. The prospect says no. You start to leave. Then you stop, as if inspired by TV's Lieutenant Colombo, and say, "Oh, one more thing. I almost forgot to mention a very important fact. If you place your order this month, you'll get one case free. You simply cannot afford to lose out on savings like that, can you?" One more thing. It works for Colombo, it will work for you.

YOUR NOTES

12. The Summarize Plus Points Close. Some prospects respond to an array of plus points marching toward them. ("It's all here in black and white. This is the best product available. You can't say no to an offer like this, can you?") Summarizing the pluses.

———————————————

YOUR NOTES

13. The Pros and Cons Close. With the analytical buyer, write out the pros and cons of your proposition, side-by-side. Naturally, you favor the pros. But give a few cons, too. Make sure the prospect agrees with each listed item. The pros and cons.

————————————

YOUR NOTES

14. The Logic Close. The buyer wants evidence. Give it in full measure. ("It must be clear to a woman of reason that, if these are your needs, this must be the right product for you. Therefore, there's only one thing for us to decide — how soon do you want these books in your library? Will next Wednesday be soon enough?") When the buyer starts answering questions about delivery, she's going to buy.

———————————————

YOUR NOTES

15. The Whispering Close. One high volume buyer says his most effective supplier whispers at the close, as if disclosing a valuable secret. Said the buyer, "I leaned forward, not wanting to miss a word. The salesman continued to whisper. I continued to follow. Before I knew it, he asked me to buy. Before I knew it, I whispered yes!"

———————————

YOUR NOTES

16. The Silent Close. One toiletries salesman doesn't say a dozen words. He merely shows merchandise. He points to this feature and that. He demonstrates. He lets the product speak. Then, he starts writing up the order and inquires, "How many?" Two words. Or, he takes out an order blank, marks an X on it, and says, "Here." One word. It works. The power of silence. Regardless of who's selling or what's being sold, most sales will continue to be closed with one, or several, classic keys. That's a science you can learn. Knowing when and how to use these keys — that's an art. It's an art that can be mastered through practice. Through time it will become natural, like an inborn reflex.

———————————————

YOUR NOTES

The nine types of customers

You've just acquired sixteen closing keys useful for what you say and how you respond in closing customers. That's half the equation in the buyer-seller communication process.

Now let's deal with the other half: What customers say — and how they respond to you.

Here are nine different customer types. Learning to spot them — and preparing to cope with them — will dramatically improve your closing average.

1. The Tribalistic Customer. Recognize these customers by their lack of personal buying values. They blindly accept beliefs and preferences of authority figures — a parent, husband, wife, or boss. To sell this prospect, be reassuring of her purchase decision — not free-wheeling, rational, or objective. Help her maintain good standing in her peer group by reinforcing the continued respect she'll receive from higher up the chain of command. The Third Party Endorsement, such as testimonials from public figures, are effective in selling Tribalistic buyers.

————————————

YOUR NOTES

2. The Egocentric Buyer. This rugged individual has become his own tribal chief. He says: "To hell with the rest of the world. I think for myself." Sometimes Mr. Egocentric believes salespeople are rip-offs. He counters by attempting to rip you off first. Anything goes in the Egocentric's effort to dominate and win. Play the game by the Egocentric's values. If he plays con man, be a better con man. If he plays tough guy, be tougher. Don't dwell on product dependability, durability, cost savings, or guarantees. Mr. Ego's more concerned about product appearance, delivery, status. He wants a product to symbolize his rugged individualism and power. Close by praising his leadership "as first in your field to take this step." Then use the Ask & Get key. Ask boldly for the order; he's a bold buyer.

———————————————

YOUR NOTES

3. Conformist Buyers. Identify the conformist by what he's not — not a high roller, not a leader. These people have difficulty accepting other values. They try to get others to accept their values — values often subordinate to a philosophy, cause, or religion. Conformists seek product dependability, durability, cost savings, guarantees, brand names from reliable, stable companies. They aren't trend-setters. They only reluctantly make changes. With the conformist, be businesslike and straightforward. Point out "everybody is buying." Dress appropriately. Avoid comments on religion, politics, or sex. Set up an exact time for the presentation and be there. Close by Summarizing Plus Points. Show it's all here in black-and-white — with proof from happy customers.

———————————

YOUR NOTES

4. Manipulative Buyers don't need assertiveness training — but they should lecture at the course. They thrive on gamesmanship, politics, competition, and antics. They measure success in possessions, status, and money. They respond to fast-paced presentations. They don't need all the details. Simply present the highlights and wait for questions. Make sure you hold some benefits in reserve — you may well need them. The manipulative customer will often play stump-the-salesperson. They'll say: "You don't mean to tell me . . ." Then they try to negotiate price. They demand a written contract with escape clauses. Your strategy: Let them believe they've won the game while you make the sale. Quietly manipulate the manipulator. Use the Something for Nothing key.

———————————————

YOUR NOTES

5. The Sociocentric Buyer values getting along over getting ahead. In dealing with a Sociocentric, relate your product or service to society. Play down status symbols, power, or materialistic gains. Talk about preservation of the environment, good taste, respectability, social responsibility, benefits to the public and to the nation. Sociocentrics prefer you as a friend, not a supplier. When you make the sale, Mr. Socio may take you to lunch. Since you've made a friend, avoid the frontal assault. Use the flanking movement with The Little Question — friend to friend.

YOUR NOTES

6. The Existential Buyer. Recognize her as a participant. She must be involved in the sale. She cannot stand by as an observer. Present the problem, give her access to information. Build a participating role for her in your demo. Emphasize problem solving. Here, price is of secondary importance. Be flexible and spontaneous. Stress simplicity and personal ethics. Avoid conventionality, status symbols, conformity, profitability, power, and short-range benefits. Let conversation flow. Don't try to force structure. Slant benefits toward acceptance of yourself, your company, your product, and its effect on the customer. Use the Do Something key. Let her operate, test, try, smell, taste. Give her a hands-on feel for the product or service.

———————————————

YOUR NOTES

7. The Dedicated Delayer. He fears being pressured or tricked into buying. He wants the last word, his self-respect and integrity intact. This prospect has been telling himself — and family or associates — he will not buy the day you present. He has built a shield around himself. He can, and does, come up with fantastic excuses for not buying, real Academy Award material. Combat the Dedicated Delayer with pros and cons on paper. Throw in Something for Nothing: "only if you OK this today."

——————————

YOUR NOTES

8. Mr. White Hat. Recognize this self-righteous personality who could have been a television evangelist. This leading man sees himself as the good guy all the way. He's going to make a decision — he has the power to grant this sale (or deny it). He's pulling all the strings. He sees you as The Black Hat. Thus, if White Hat stretches the truth or misleads Black Hat, it's all fair. Play to the ego. Congratulate him on his judgment. Use the Win/Win Choice key. Don't ask if, ask which. Play the game until you can say: "Please put your initials right here, Mr. White Hat. You have the right slant on this problem."

YOUR NOTES

9. The Greedy Customer often starts by saying "I can get a better buy someplace else." She wants the best deal possible and she'll use every trick to get it. This buyer — not dishonest exactly — wants to use her money to fullest advantage. Come up with a bottom-lineoriented close to feed the greedy. Since she's for profit and savings, offer her both. Ask: "Do you want the greater savings from a two-year payment plan or the greater convenience of a three-year plan?" Also throw in the Coming Event. Let her know the deal is only available until next Thursday. There you have nine customer-types. When you go in armed with this psychological edge, combined with the right closers, you start with a powerful advantage.

——————————————

YOUR NOTES

The Sales Objections!

"I don't know your company."

What client means

"Who are you?"

Clients have found that purely "emotional" objections like this one quickly uncover the insecurities of average salespeople.

Average salesperson

Thinks: *"No you don't. Why does no-one like me?"*

Action: Becomes defensive, waffles and ultimately bails out of the call.

———————————————

YOUR NOTES

"Fantastic! That's exactly why I've called. We're the ... (give opening statement or unique selling points)."

Sales Superstar

Thinks: *"You will in a minute!"*

Understands: Peak performers are motivated from the inside out. Only average sales people are affected by this kind of comment.

Why this works

- It reframes the client's expectations of how salespeople behave
- It's positive and amusing
- It was never a real objection anyway!

———————————————

YOUR NOTES

"We don't use that!"

What client means

"I see no need for your services."

This client either does not see the need for your services or is using this approach as an instant conversation terminator.

Average salesperson

Thinks: *"No-one wants our products!"*

Action: Either bails out of the call or gets confrontational and pushes against the client's resistance.

——————————————

YOUR NOTES

"And I'm not asking you to change now, merely get to know you and understand a little more about your business and what you do use."

Sales Superstar

Thinks: "And I'll find a need for it if you have one!"

Understands: The parable of the two shoe salespeople in Africa. One messages back, "Bring me home, no-one wears shoes out here", the other messages back, "Send more shoes! No-one wears shoes out here!"

Why this works

- Defuses "threat" of the pushy salesperson
- "Change now" is an embedded command
- Who doesn't like to talk about themselves and their business?

YOUR NOTES

"All of that is controlled by head office in the USA."

What client means

"It's not in my control."

Client does not want to waste time talking about something that is not within his control. It's also a great way of getting rid of unwanted salespeople!

Average salesperson

Thinks: "Why is nothing as easy as it used to be?"

Action: Bails out of the call and adds to their collection of negative sales memories.

YOUR NOTES

"Where in the US?

Who looks after it?

What's his / her role? What's their phone number?

When was that implemented?

(And gradually move into...)

How effective has it been?

What were the business reasons for implementing that in the first place?"

Sales Superstar

Thinks: *"You can't stop me that easily!"*

Understands: Building business relationships in today's markets is like putting together the many pieces of a complex puzzle. Only by building many lines of communication can the picture be completed.

Why this works

- Uses "misdirection" to gather information and lets client think that you're asking standard sales questions. This helps them to relax and allows you to build deeper rapport
- You then move to deeper questions so that you can uncover needs and opportunities

---

YOUR NOTES

"I'm afraid that area of the business is outsourced."

What client means

"Not today!"

In today's markets, outsourcing areas of the business is becoming increasingly popular with companies seeking to reduce overheads, cut costs and maximise profits. Ordinary salespeople are too focused on products and not commercially minded enough to understand the potential opportunities here.

Average salesperson

Thinks: *"I could have been somebody! This market is rubbish!"*

Action: Thanks client and departs with another notch on their *"woe is me"* belt.

———————————

YOUR NOTES

"That's fine. As someone focused on providing specialist solutions in that area I'm pleased that you take it so seriously. I'm curious, what were your reasons for outsourcing that area of your business in the first place?"

Sales Superstar

Thinks: *"We'll see about that!"*

Understands: As fast as one area is outsourced another is brought back in-house. Careful investigation may uncover alternative opportunities, "middle-man" deals and even problems in the existing outsourcing solution.

Why this works

• Positions you as an expert

• Respects client's position

• *"I'm curious"* is a real "softener" • Links nicely to questions

———————————————

YOUR NOTES

"I haven't enough time."

What client means

"I'm busy and you'd better not waste my time."

This kind of objection usually means that the client is busy and that they get a lot of sales calls. It's really not personal but most salespeople take it this way!

Average salesperson

Thinks: *"I'll be as quick as possible then!"*

Action: Makes excuses for the call, rushes into the pitch and gets rejected. When salespeople rush in this way it sends a psychological message that they are not important and therefore not worth dealing with.

YOUR NOTES

Attempt 1:

"And I won't waste a moment of your time."

Attempt 2 (if he repeats himself):

"I apologise. When this week would be more convenient to call?

How would Friday afternoon be for you? 3 or 4pm?"

(Book call or meeting)

Sales Superstar

Thinks: *"I am worthy of your time."*

Understands: All clients make time for the right sales conversations therefore the key here is to maintain composure and differentiate your call as being worthy of the client's time. Ensure that you control your pace, tone and pitch.

Why this works

- The initial acknowledgement is enough for most clients
- Takes responsibility if the client repeats the objection
- Sets a time for the conversation using different closing techniques

---

YOUR NOTES

"You're too expensive!"

What client means

"I reckon I can get a bargain here."

The "price" objection is one of the most feared by salespeople and clients know it! What's more they are not afraid to use it liberally.

Average salesperson

Thinks: *"Quick! Give him a discount – I'm too expensive!"*

Action: Reduces price, appears desperate, throws away an opportunity.

———————————

YOUR NOTES

Option 1: "I'm sure you have a good reason for saying that, do you mind me asking you what it is?"

Option 2: "Are you considering the price or the total cost of ownership? Certainly when you look at the price on a piece of paper we're not the cheapest. When you consider the total cost of ownership which includes ... (name client's needs / criteria) ... then you will be able to see that we provide the best return on investment."

Option 3: "Well, I certainly don't mind people selling for less. However, and you will understand why I ask you this, how important is it that any purchase provides a return on investment? Why? And you know that's exactly why..."

Sales Superstar

Thinks: *"You've just not understood the value yet!"*

Understands: Clients are always going to try and negotiate and most aren't that serious about it anyway. If they are the Sales Superstar will ask questions to build the value before negotiating.

Why this works

- Shows empathy
- Uncovers real costs not just figures
- Reframes the client's perspective

- Shows confidence and professionalism

YOUR NOTES

"I'm happy with my current suppliers thank you."

What client means

"I get these calls all of the time."

Clients have found that most sales people have no useful answer to this objection! They often use it without any consideration as to whether they really are happy or not.

Average salesperson

Thinks: *"Everyone has a supplier already! Why do I bother with this job?"*

Action: Bails out of the call or challenges for a weakness in the client's existing relationships. This usually results in confrontation.

——————————————

YOUR NOTES

Attempt 1:

"Great and I'm not asking you to change now merely consider building a relationship..."

Attempt 2:

"Many of my other clients told me the same thing. They were also working with existing suppliers before they realised that our service perfectly complemented what they were already doing. I'd like to get together and show you how..."

Sales Superstar

Thinks: *"Really! We'll see about that!"*

Understands: It has been estimated that only 5% of clients are genuinely "happy" with their current suppliers but most won't tell you until you've got significant amounts of trust and rapport.

Why this works

• Does not challenge or threaten the existing supplier relationship

• Respects the client's decision

• *"Change now"* is an embedded command • Uses inclusive approach with the word *"complemented"*

————————————

YOUR NOTES

"We've got a preferred supplier's list!"

What client means

"Not today thank you!"

In some industries this objection is the most feared objection that there is. Clients know this and produce it with a flourish leaving a trail of battered salespeople in their wake!

Average salesperson

Thinks: *"Not again! I hate this job!"*

Action: Asks when the list is up for renewal, sends some literature and books a call-back for some "more appropriate" time in the future.

———————————————

YOUR NOTES

"I'm pleased to hear that! Many of our partner companies have preferred supplier's lists as well. I'm sure that you had good business reasons for setting that up. Do you mind telling me, what were they?"

Sales Superstar

Thinks: *"And I know that you don't always use it!"*

Understands: Clients virtually always source some services / products outside of their existing supplier relationships. Getting onto the list requires a long-term strategy so there are two different angles here – one for the short-term and one for the long-term.

Why this works

• Acknowledges client's position

• Reframes salesperson's position as a partner • Links to information seeking questions

——————————————

YOUR NOTES

"We're about to be taken over."

What client means

"I'm in trouble and this is bad timing."

This client may be feeling very vulnerable right now. He won't be wanting to speak with brash sales people.

Average salesperson

Thinks: *"There by the grace of God go I!"*

Action: Feels embarrassed, sees no opportunity, exits the call or (far worse) pushes to try to expose needs right now in a very unsubtle manner!

——————————————

YOUR NOTES

"I'm sorry to hear that, those situations are always challenging ... (move to questions about the take over)."

Sales Superstar

Thinks: *"Poor chap. Maybe I can help."*

Understands: Measured empathy can go a long way right now. In the future this client may end up being promoted in the turmoil or may even end up winning a more influential position elsewhere.

Why this works

- Shows professional empathy and builds rapport
- *"Those"* linguistically distances both of you from the situation slightly
- Moving to questions builds rapport
- Allows you to judge the next step carefully

———————————————

YOUR NOTES

"We're making redundancies at the moment."

What client means

"Have you no sensitivity?"

This client is either worrying about his own job or is buried in the middle of a very difficult management scenario. A pushy, proactive salesperson talking about opportunities and requirements is not on his agenda!

Average salesperson

Thinks: *"I can't believe it. What a waste of my time!"*

Action: Gives up, feels bad, takes a step closer to another wasted day in the office!

———————————————

YOUR NOTES

"I'm sorry to hear that – it's never easy to make business decisions like that. When you consider the importance of any strategic decision like that it is essential to have the right support systems in place. It may be that we can help, tell me..."

Sales Superstar

Thinks: *"I wonder what opportunities may lie within those business challenges?"*

Understands: Companies always have business reasons for making decisions like this whether due to increased technology or difficult market conditions. Maybe the Sales Superstar can provide a solution to one of the problems. In any case, most companies expand again at some point.

Why this works

- Empathises with client's situation
- Demonstrates strategic business awareness
- Reframes client perspective from problems to solutions and moves into any question that you believe appropriate

____

YOUR NOTES

"It's the end of the financial year at the moment. We can't look at anything until the new financial year."

What client means

"I'm really busy. Go away."

This objection could well be the truth or it could well be a fabrication. In any case, this client is using an objection which works wonders on most salespeople. The client just knows how they are going to respond!

Average salesperson

Thinks: *"Great! He's interested! I'll call back in the new financial year!"*

Action: Asks when the new financial year begins and books a call back into his database for then. Sadly, you could spend whole sales careers ringing back clients like this one with little chance of a deal.

——————————————

YOUR NOTES

"That's good news because I wasn't wanting to show you anything right now just introduce myself and gain a greater understanding of you and your business. Tell me ... (move to questions)."

Sales Superstar

Thinks: *"Oh really! Let's see what we can do about that!"*

Understands: Business doesn't stop for 3 months prior to the end of the financial year like many clients claim. If the client can't see any value in you and your proposition right now why will he be able to do so in 3 months time? More information is needed from the client.

Why this works

- Reframes client's expectations with the opening statement
- *"Because"* creates a subconscious link to a totally reasonable objective of introducing yourself
- *"You and your"* shows interest in the client

———————————————

YOUR NOTES

"I've got no budget."

Client means

"I've got no budget for you."

Clients know that 95% of salespeople will ask when they do have a budget and arrange to call them back then. What a great way of getting rid of salespeople!

Average salesperson

Thinks: *"This job is rubbish, the market's rubbish; no-one ever has any budget."*

Action: Becomes disconsolate, fails to build rapport and creates a weak pipeline.

———————————

YOUR NOTES

"Thanks for sharing that with me. When I first spoke to them many of my clients didn't have budgets and that's what makes us different. At this point most companies would probably ask when you do have a budget and not talk now. We at ... (name company) ... believe in building strong relationships with our clients and I'd like to invest in getting to know you now."

Sales Superstar

Thinks: *"Not yet you haven't."*

Understands: Most salespeople will bail out of this call here so this is a great opportunity to build a relationship and win a client that others have ignored. Also, most clients can create or reallocate budgets if they perceive a big enough need.

Why this works

• Acknowledges client's situation

• Uses a 3rd party experience to reframe the situation

• *"Talk now"* is an embedded command

• *"Invest in"* the client is flattering

———————————————

YOUR NOTES

"Is this a sales call?"

What client means

"Are you a waste of space?"

Many clients get dozens of calls a day from unprofessional salespeople from which they develop beliefs and perceptions about the value of salespeople in society. Giving salespeople a hard time can (at some level) also make clients feel better about themselves!

Average salesperson

Thinks: *"Oh no! I've been sussed again! If only I'd have worked harder at school!"*

Action: Makes excuses, talks too quickly, appears unconfident and, unsurprisingly, gets rejected.

——————————————

YOUR NOTES

"Yes / No / or Well ... (you choose which!) The reason for my call is to introduce myself and my company..."

Sales Superstar

Thinks: *"You'd better believe it!"* **Understands:** Dealing with other people's insecurities is part of the role of a sales professional. No one can detract from the Sales Superstar's belief that he provides a valuable service to his clients.

Why this works

- Answers the question!
- Takes control in a professional manner
- Implies the importance of the call via the style of the delivery

———————————————

YOUR NOTES

"I've got no need."

What client means

"No thanks!"

Logically, this is the most obvious of objections but it is not used as much as it might be by clients because of its somewhat direct nature. As such, if it is used it is usually by fairly direct clients who like to get to the point, fast!

Average salesperson

Thinks: *"Another one! Why is it that no-one has any need for me?"*

Action: Gives up and exits the call or tries to convince the client that they either do have a need or that they would have one if they knew how great the salesperson's solution / product was. Either option equals resistance.

YOUR NOTES

"And I'm not asking you to buy now John, merely keep your self appraised of opportunities available in the market right now. Tell me John..."

Sales Superstar

Thinks: *"At last! An opportunity worthy of my sales abilities!"*

Understands: The vast majority of salespeople are "order-takers" dealing only with clients who are well advanced in the sales process. Sales Superstars help their clients to implement solutions which will help their businesses now and in the future.

Why this works

• Avoids pushing against a "closed door"

• Is full of embedded commands – *"buy now",*

"keep yourself appraised" and "right now" • Links to questions

———————————

YOUR NOTES

"I don't want whatever it is!"

Client means

"I'm busy and I've had a lot of calls lately."

This client is exasperated with the numbers of calls that they are getting. This all-encompassing blanket objection is designed to terminate any and all sales calls as fast as possible.

Average salesperson

Thinks: *"Not surprised! No-one ever does!"*

Action: Puts on his "sales" hat and tries to "sell" the client on his product. At best this will result in a swift exit from the call!!

———————————————

YOUR NOTES

"And I certainly won't try to sell anything to you now. The reason for my call is to introduce myself and my company..."

Sales Superstar

Thinks: *"Lets rock 'n 'roll!"*

Understands: This client has to make their purchases somewhere and with an approach like that most salespeople will have fallen at the first hurdle. Its time for the Sales Superstar to make their move!

Why this works

• It's not much of an objection really so it will more than likely just go away once you don't rise to the bait!

• Links back to relationship building

——————————————

YOUR NOTES

"Just give me the price."

What client means

"Get it over with and I can tell you to go away."

This client is taking control and trying to rush the salesperson to the point where they can reject them. Most salespeople will just give the price and leave the client to their own decision making process.

Average salesperson

Thinks: *"Here comes a price rejection and we'll be too expensive."*

Action: Gives the price in a very defensive and unconfident manner, precipitates a price objection and fails to win the sale.

———————————

YOUR NOTES

"I certainly will do. However, as you would expect there are various different solutions available. In order to make sure that you get the best return on investment and the right solution I need to ask you some questions. From that I'll give you the best price. Tell me John... "

Sales Superstar

Thinks: *"Woah there boy! Not until I've established a big enough need!"*

Understands: Average salespeople invite their own objections by quoting prices too early in the sales process. Sales Superstars deal with potential objections before they surface. They ensure that the client has a strong need prior to talking figures.

Why this works

- Agrees with request
- Everyone wants the *"best price"*
- Reframes price as *"investment"*
- Links to questions about the business

———————————————

YOUR NOTES

"We don't take cold calls."

What client means

"We're too important to talk to you!"

In an effort to reduce time wasting and increase profitability some companies have introduced clearly unenforceable policies such as this. Despite the ambiguity of this comment, it's more than enough of an obstacle for most salespeople.

Average salesperson

Thinks: *"And that's what I do isn't it! What a useless job!"*

Action: Exits call, argues or becomes desperate. Not good!

———————————

YOUR NOTES

"That's fine because the reason for my call is to introduce myself and my company..."

Sales Superstar

Thinks: *"You just did!"*

Understands: Selling is a serious profession that provides unrivalled career opportunities to the best players. Cold calling plays an important part in the Sales Superstar's toolkit.

Why this works

- None confrontational
- Agrees with client then links with word *"because"* to a reframing of the client's perspective about the call

——————————————

YOUR NOTES

"Haven't you anything better to do?"

What client means

"I'm having a bad day and I'm taking it out on you!"

This put down is a deliberate blow aimed at the salesperson's confidence. It's likely to come from clients who are having a bad day and is very effective in getting rid of sales people.

Average salesperson

Thinks: *"No."*

Action: Feels really bad about themselves and then becomes really defensive about their role and their job. Usually gabbles a lot!

———————————

YOUR NOTES

Option 1:

Totally ignore the objection all together and carry on

with the call. "Actually the reason for the call..."

Option 2:

"That's a very philosophical question and one which I'll happily discuss another time. The reason for my call today is..."

Sales Superstar

Thinks: *"What could be better than selling?"* **Understands:** A Sales Superstar is 100% responsible for managing their own internal state irrespective of the actions of anyone around them. A meaningless question like this will not effect them in any way whatsoever.

Why this works

- This objection deserves little airtime
- 2nd option is humorous yet makes a serious point
- Respects client's position and gets to the point

——————————————

YOUR NOTES

"Look! There's a war on!"

(Or similar)

What client means

"Go away."

If your client intends to remain in business then they must purchase things to be able to run their business. This is either an excuse or a failure to realise the consequences of not continuing to invest in their business.

Average salesperson

Thinks: "You don't have to tell me. I'm the one selling nothing."

Action: Becomes apologetic or desperate.

———————————

YOUR NOTES

"I know! That's exactly why I've called. When the market's picked up and we look back at this moment we'll know what a great time it is to build relationships and partnerships for the future."

Sales Superstar

Thinks: *"And?"*

Understands: Sales Superstars help clients to understand and develop their businesses by providing solutions to existing and future problems. Most clients need just as much (if not more) help in a difficult market.

Why this works

- Starts with a surprise agreement
- Uses time distortion to bring the current market problems into perspective
- Aligns client and salesperson together verbally

———————————————

YOUR NOTES

"Are you trying to sell me something?"

What client means

"Here we go! Another pushy sales pitch!"

This type of emotional objection has no real substance and is purely designed to make you feel bad. It could be the result of the client having a bad day, a bad experience or having deep-rooted psychological problems! In any case, it usually does the trick and gets rid of the salesperson.

Average salesperson

Thinks: *"Yes, I am and I know that I'm just a salesperson! Please don't rub it in!"*

Action: Uncovers the salesperson's personal insecurities causing them to become defensive.

——————————————

YOUR NOTES

"Yes / no / or well ... the reason for this call is to..."

Sales Superstar

Thinks: *"Not yet! But I will!"*

Understands: Most emotional objections simply disappear when the sales person demonstrates that they have no impact. Controlled pace, clarity and authority are important in the delivery of this reply.

Why this works

- Personal choice of answers
- All answer the client's question
- Sales Superstar remains unemotional and professional

—————————————

YOUR NOTES

"I've heard bad things about your company / product."

What client means

"I'm not sure about you."

Today's markets move very quickly and news travels very rapidly. Whether real or unreal, fact or fiction clients will often think that they have heard something negative about your company.

Average salesperson

Thinks: *"Not another one. How have we upset so many people?"*

Action: Starts to explain either how good the company is now or how things have changed within the company. The first option is too pushy and the second is likely to create more objections!

——————————————

YOUR NOTES

"I'm sorry to hear that, we certainly pride ourselves on our unrivalled reputation. Tell me (name client), what have you heard? (Listen!)

I'm sorry about that, how would you like me to resolve this now so that we can move things forward?"

Sales Superstar

Thinks: *"I'm sure that I can help you to feel good about working with us!"*

Understands:

1) This is probably going to be a misunderstanding.

2) Some statistics show that 90%+ of complainants simply want to be listened to and to receive an apology.

Why this works

• Takes personal responsibility with the apology

• Listens to what happened

• Moves to a resolution *"now"* and understands that 90%+ of clients don't want anything more than the apology

——————————————

YOUR NOTES

"This is my 20th call today!"

What client means

"Don't waste my time."

This client is probably busy and doesn't want to waste time with irrelevant sales calls.

Average salesperson

Thinks: *"Oh dear! I'm a beggar!"*

Action: Rushing, unconfident, and apologetic the average performer quickly loses momentum and fails again!

———————————————

YOUR NOTES

Attempt 1:

"Well, I won't waste a moment of your time..."

Attempt 2:

"You know and that's exactly why I'm calling. It's not always convenient to take those types of calls. One of the things that we have done for partners is help to reduce them. In order to help to do that I need to..."

Sales Superstar

Thinks: *"And it might be your lucky day!"* **Understands:** People run repetitive and habitual patterns of behaviour and this client needs their pattern interrupting!

Why this works

- Attempt 1 side-steps the objection
- Attempt 2 understands the client's perspective
- *"Those"* linguistically distinguishes you from the 20 calls
- Links to your next steps

———————————

YOUR NOTES

"Go away!"

(Or worse!)

What client means

"Go away! I'm busy."

Objections like this one are reasonably rare although they do occur from time to time. As a rule most people are basically polite and this kind of objection usually manages to incense average salespeople.

Average salesperson

Thinks: *"How rude! Why do I have to be spoken to like this?"*

Action: Either exits the call fast or becomes confrontational. Not a great starting point for a relationship. Contrary to what most salespeople say, venting their emotions does not normally lead to a more resourceful state afterwards either!

———————————

YOUR NOTES

"I certainly can do (name client) although there are several key factors prevalent in the market at the moment that could well be of interest to you. Tell me, how important is it to stay abreast of what's going on in the market right now?"

Sales Superstar

Thinks: *"Curious! I wonder what upset him?"* **Understands:** Nothing has any meaning other than the meaning that we give to it therefore the Sales Superstar knows that he can choose how to interpret any situation. It may not be possible to deal with this client right now but the Sales Superstar is going to have a good try!

Why this works

- 1st try politely reframes client's experience
- 2nd try offers a "carrot" then moves to a question which it is hard to answer in the negative
- Using client's name makes it psychologically more difficult for them to be difficult again

———————————————

YOUR NOTES

"We've just bought one of those."

What client means

"We already have a supplier so we have no need."

People often do look at things in black and white terms such as right versus wrong, up versus down and need versus no need. In any case, this simple objection gets rid of 90%+ of salespeople.

Average salesperson

Thinks: *"No-one ever needs me. How come I'm never lucky?"*

Action: Leaves call a loser or fights with the client about the validity of their recent purchase. Would you listen to someone who doesn't know you and your business telling you that you've not made the best decision?

———————————————

YOUR NOTES

"I'm sorry we weren't there to help that time. The reason for my call was actually to..."

Sales Superstar

Thinks: *"Great! So my information about you being a potential client was right!"*

Understands: Pushing against a closed door now would be foolish. All clients at some point assess the solution that they have implemented, the logistics of that purchase and the impact of any changes. Building a relationship now puts our Sales Superstar in pole position when doubt or future need comes along.

Why this works

• Takes responsibility

• *"That time"* puts the event into the past and moves the conversation forwards

• If the client objects again it will more than likely be a different objection e.g. no need.

———————————

YOUR NOTES

"Does he know what the call's regarding?"

What client means

"I think that you're a salesperson."

Something has identified you as a salesperson and this person's role is to block sales calls. For most salespeople, gatekeepers are a major problem in their ability to get through to decision-makers. This is good news for clients who are trying to avoid sales calls and bad news for salespeople who want to make new contacts!

Average salesperson

Thinks: *"Oh no! Not this again!"*

Action: Gets confrontational!

——————————————

YOUR NOTES

"My name is ____, ____________, the leading supplier of ____________________. I work with senior managers to help them to increase turnover and maximise profitability in the sales arena. As you know, there are various competitive factors prevalent in the market at the moment that (name client) will be strategically aware of. If you could just let him know that I'm on the line. Thank you."

Sales Superstar

Thinks: "It's only a question and how I answer it

will dictate my success."

Understands: A change of tack is necessary here to differentiate the importance of your call. It's also worth looking at your opening statement if this is occurring frequently as something that you are doing is probably inviting this reaction from gatekeepers.

Why this works

- Implies first name terms
- Strategic element suggests seniority
- *"As you know"* is inclusive of the "blocker"
- Final line is a polite order
- "Blocker" wouldn't want to not put through someone that they should be putting through!

——————————————

YOUR NOTES

"Can I say who's calling?"

What client means

"Is this a sales call?"

Client believes that this is a sales call and is looking for confirmation in order to end the call. Much like the last scenario this innocent question is the beginning of a nightmare for many salespeople!

Average salesperson

Thinks: *"Busted!"*

Action: Approaches this question with a poor attitude and low in confidence. This usually ends in an equally dismal outcome!

———————————————

YOUR NOTES

"Yes, of course. If you could just let him know that it's ______, ________________ on the line for him. Thank you."

Sales Superstar

Thinks: *"I'm not falling for that!"*

Understands: "Blockers" are only doing their job and they will put through the calls that they need to! Belief, confidence and voice coaching all play a major part in dealing with gatekeepers successfully.

Why this works

• Answers question politely but firmly

• Minimises the request with a polite order • Implies first name terms

———————————————

YOUR NOTES

"Speak to my PA."

What client means

"I'm too important to speak to you."

Clients habitually pass sales calls on to personal assistants because they don't see the value in having the conversation themselves. As an objection this works because many salespeople are relieved that they don't have to speak with a director!

Average salesperson

Thinks: *"No-one wants to speak with me and now I'm going to have to fight with the PA!"*

Action: Accepts this ploy and then gets into a power struggle with the PA.

——————————————

YOUR NOTES

"Thanks, I certainly can do. I work with senior decision makers like yourself and I specifically rang today to meet you. My name's ________ and my company is the premier ________________________..."

Sales Superstar

Thinks: *"You must be joking!"*

Understands: Building relationships with PA's is and can be vital to the success of a sale but this is not the time. At best the PA will listen and make a decision, at worst reject you. This call needs to be repositioned – fast!

Why this works

• *"Senior managers like you"* is flattering but also repositions the call

• The objection handle roles seamlessly back into the call

• Demonstrates polite, directorial style control

———————————————

YOUR NOTES

"I'm in the middle of something right now!"

What client means

"I'm in the middle of something right now!"

Although this statement could be a lie (just like *"He's in a meeting"*) we need to "accept" that this statement is true. As an objection it works for clients as salespeople normally go away, often not to return.

Average salesperson

Thinks: *"Liar! Everyone always tries to avoid me."*

Action: Tries to move ahead with the call thus creating resistance. Notably, this approach is likely to create resistance whether the client's initial statement was true or not.

——————————————

YOUR NOTES

"Sorry to have disturbed you. When would be more convenient to talk? (Later in the week)

Thursday or Friday, which would be

best for you?

(Friday)

Morning or afternoon?

(Morning)

10 or 11 am, which would you prefer?"

Sales Superstar

Thinks: *"OK. Then let's schedule a time that's more convenient for both of us."*

Understands: Treating this objection as true is the only professional option. The primary objective now is to schedule another call with the client. If the objection is a "lie" it may "disappear" during the scheduling process.

Why this works

• Respectful and courteous

• "Funnel" closes the client to an agreed time and date

• The only way out of this for the client is to give you the go ahead to talk to them now (i.e. *"What's the call regarding?"*)

——————————————

YOUR NOTES

"You need to speak to the human resources department."

What client means

"I see no value in speaking to you."

This client doesn't see the value in speaking with you and believes that this area of the business is / should be dealt with elsewhere.

Average salesperson

Thinks: *"Here we go again! Passed down to someone else like always."*

Action: Either departs "cap in hand" for the HR department or starts to "fight" this decision.

—————————————

YOUR NOTES

"I certainly will do that then, thank you. In order that I understand your business better and so that I can provide the best service to you through them tell me (name client), what is the business advantage of working in that manner?"

Sales Superstar

Thinks: *"OK but now I'm here I'm going to get the most out of this call that I possibly can!"* **Understands:** Many companies and decision-makers pass suppliers to non-decision making, non-outcome, orientated departments or individuals. Dealing with these departments is strategically important for long-term supplier partnerships but having a strong business relationship with key decision-makers is vital too.

Why this works

- Agrees to client's request

- Makes a clever statement which validates the need for the client to answer the question coming up

- Seeks out the key business needs and decision making strategies and starts a conversation

———————————————

YOUR NOTES

"I'm already talking to a couple of suppliers about this."

What client means

"I'm in purchasing mode but I've no time to waste."

This client believes that the chances are that you'll waste his time. With most salespeople he's probably right too! This comment will send all but the Sales Superstars into a bit of a desperate panic.

Average salesperson

Thinks: *"I can't believe I've missed another opportunity."*

Action: Either bails out of the call or becomes desperate neither of which will result in the opportunity to work with this client.

——————————————

YOUR NOTES

"Good. It's certainly important that any business decision such as this is researched properly and therefore that you're talking to the most compatible suppliers. Tell me, what were your business reasons for looking at (the problem or the solution) in the first place? (Get answers)

And that's exactly why... "

Sales Superstar

Thinks: *"Great! A hot lead. Bring it on!"* **Understands:** This client is going to buy and has already completed the initial qualification process. To take a seat at the table the Sales Superstar must build rapid rapport, understand the client's business drivers and represent a credible option.

Why this works

• Demonstrates a strategic understanding of business relationships and needs

• Uncovers business drivers and links them to you and your solution

———————————

YOUR NOTES

"Call back in 3 months."

What this means

"Get lost!"

Many clients, particularly people-orientated ones, have found that sounding interested and asking salespeople to call back is a great way of getting them off the line and avoiding any confrontation.

Average salesperson

Thinks: *"He like me but he has no need. I don't want to push too hard and upset him."*

Action: Ditches the call for fear of losing "the deal". Books a callback into the database and fills his "pipeline" with another weak call.

YOUR NOTES

"Thanks for asking me to! At this point I guess most companies would schedule a call back for 3 months time. We at (name company) pride ourselves on working in partnership with our clients and I'd like to invest the time in meeting you now so that in 3 months time I'm in the best place to help you."

Sales Superstar

Thinks: *"Not unless I have a real reason to pal!"* **Understands:** This client needs qualifying before they're worthy of a callback. Nice people don't necessarily make the best clients!

Why this works

- Agrees with the client and is non-threatening
- Identifies that a "real" potential partner wouldn't just ring off and call back in 3 months time

———————————————

YOUR NOTES

"You've got two minutes."

What client means

"Please don't waste my time like that last idiot!"

This client is trying to take control of the call and, what's more, on 95% of occasions will probably succeed. This time challenge is all too much for most "brow-beaten" salespeople!

Average salesperson

Thinks: *"I've interrupted him. He doesn't want to talk with me. I'd better hurry up."*

Action: Apologises for calling, rushes, mumbles, asks negative questions, expects to fail and does!

YOUR NOTES

"Thank you. The reason for my call is..."

Sales Superstar

Thinks: *"That's all I need to get you wanting more!"*

Understands: People make a decision about you within seconds of speaking to you therefore this client will know within two minutes whether he wants to know more or not. First impressions count!

Why this works

- Acknowledges comment and takes control
- Is professional not emotional
- Delivery, pace and confidence imply seniority and importance

———————————————

YOUR NOTES

"I don't like you!"

What client means

"I don't like salespeople!"

Let's face it some clients are just down right rude at times! This client may be having a bad day or perhaps he's just obnoxious; in any case he's going to take it out on you!

Average salesperson

Thinks: *"I don't like me either!"*

Action: Feels bad, visualises a few negative memories, makes excuses and leaves the call.

——————————————

YOUR NOTES

"Then it's a good job I don't get emotional about building mutually beneficial business opportunities! The reason for my call is to..."

Sales Superstar

Thinks: *"Grow up!"*

Understands: This client doesn't even know you! Most salespeople will duck out of this call early on so what a great challenge for the Sales Superstar to turn it around!

Why this works

• Very tongue in cheek

• It reframes the situation and reminds the client of where they are (i.e. work!)

• It's professional and moves straight back to the call structure

———————————————

YOUR NOTES

"Send me literature."

What client means

"Go away!"

Clients have found that this is a really easy way to get rid of salespeople who are more than willing to send emails and literature because it gets them off the phone whilst they are doing it!

Average salesperson

Thinks: *"Yes, OK."*

Action: Takes the easy way out and misses an opportunity.

——————————————

YOUR NOTES

"I certainly will do that (and I'm pleased that you're interested in our company). As you may expect, we have a large amount of company literature. In order that it exactly meets your needs what I'd like to do is ask a few questions (come and meet with you) and from there I'll happily select the information which matches your needs."

Sales Superstar

Thinks: *"Most of my competitors will miss out here so this is a great opportunity."* **Understands:** Literature at this stage would more than likely end up in the bin. Clients buy based on their problems, challenges and needs; failure to take the time to understand these buys only a ticket for a lottery!

Why this works

- Agrees with client's request
- Respects that he is busy
- Links to asking about him and his business

———————————

YOUR NOTES

"What's the call regarding?"

What this client means

"Don't mess about pal!"

This is another unassuming phrase that sorts the wheat from the chaff as far as salespeople are concerned. By rights, it shouldn't be an objection but in practise it is!

Average salesperson

Thinks: *"He's onto me. He thinks that I'm a two- bob, second hand car dealer at heart!"*

Action: Feels pressurised and starts to blab about not wasting the client's time. Upshot? Wastes client's time!

——————————————

YOUR NOTES

"The reason for my call is to..."

Sales Superstar

Thinks: *"You asked for it!"*

Understands: This client just asked you what the call's regarding? Do you get a greener green light than that? Err ... no! Watch pace, tone, confidence and energy levels as you approach the call.

Why this works

- Confident and professional
- It's what the client asked for!
- It was never really an objection anyway!

———————————————

YOUR NOTES

"Why should I speak to you?"

What the client means

"I get a lot of sales calls. Don't waste my time."

Clients know that this question puts all but the best salespeople onto the back foot. From the client's perspective it's very easy to take any answer that the salesperson gives and say that it's not a good enough reason to talk to them!

Average salesperson

Thinks: *"I don't know."*

Action: Desperately dumps heaps of information as fast as possible in the hope of hitting the mark! Too often they don't.

——————————————

YOUR NOTES

"You know that's a great question and there certainly are many business reasons why my clients do speak with me. Tell me, why wouldn't you speak to me?"

Sales Superstar

Thinks: *"I don't know yet but there are plenty of reasons so let's find them together!"* **Understands:** Most clients don't really want a reason to talk, they want a reason not to! Our Sales Superstar will get underneath this objection and uncover the client's real needs and wants.

Why this works

• Acknowledges the client's question

• Links to *"business reasons"* and create credibility by mention of other *"clients"*

• Starts to uncover any real objections and / or drivers

——————————————

YOUR NOTES

"I'm not the right person."

What client means

"I'm not talking to you."

This is an interesting objection, as experience would suggest that this objection is often untrue. It is also irrefutable so it ends calls virtually instantaneously.

Average salesperson

Thinks: *"More duff info! Our database really is rubbish."*

Action: Asks who is the right person to talk to and exits the call thus missing an opportunity; not to mention going on what will probably be a "wild goose chase"!

———————————————

YOUR NOTES

Option 1: "At this point I guess most

people would ask you who the decision maker is and hang up and call them but I believe that business is built on relationships and I would like to take the time to get to know you. Tell me..."

Option 2: "Sorry about that, I thought that

you were, my mistake. Who should I be speaking with? What is his / her role? What department is he / she in? What's the number? Thank you for all of your help. I wonder if you could help me a little more – tell me, what ... (move to whatever questions it would be useful for you to know)."

Sales Superstar

Thinks: *"I don't mind, I'm going to talk to you now we're speaking."*

Understands: This client could be lying or he could be telling the truth! Either way he could well hold the key to the puzzle of unlocking this account. A Sales Superstar aims to maximise his results from every sales call or visit.

Why this works

- Option 1 – most people are happy to say hello
- Option 2 - takes responsibility and uses misdirection

- Eventually the misdirection leads to information gathering questions

———————————————

YOUR NOTES

"I need more time to make a decision."

What client means

"There's something that I'm not telling you."

This tactic is used a lot by clients who either aren't the only decision-maker, who find it hard to make decisions or have some kind of hidden objection. The problem from the salesperson's perspective is that once a deal starts to slow down they often stop altogether!

Average salesperson

Thinks: *"He doesn't want it! Is there a competitor sniffing around? Was it too expensive?"*

Action: Focuses on not losing a deal that hasn't even been won yet! Often cuts the price or offers a discount thus starting a price war or negotiation.

——————————————

YOUR NOTES

"Thanks for sharing that with me John. I'm happy to give you any information and answer any questions that you may have to help you to decide now. It's certainly important that you've made the right decision. Tell me John, what are the key factors upon which you are deciding?"

Sales Superstar

Thinks: *"I need to find out more about what you are deciding upon."*

Understands: A decision is not a static thing that just happens; a client needs to go through a "decision making process". A Sales Superstar becomes part of this process thus helping, influencing and coaching the client.

Why this works

• Demonstrates verbally that it is a process • *"Decide now"* and *"you've made the right decision"* are both embedded commands

• The question starts to uncover the factors most important in the decision making process

——————————————

YOUR NOTES

"I haven't received it yet."

What client means

"I haven't received it yet!"

Not really an objection this one but it could be a stall for more time so it has to be dealt with. This only really works as an objection because of the emotional effect it has on some salespeople.

Average salesperson

Thinks: *"He's probably lying."*

Action: Feels irritated and sounds accusatory. Clearly, this doesn't lead to a great call.

———————————

YOUR NOTES

"I'm sorry about that. Our literature is extensive anyway so what I'd like to do is tailor some specific information just for you and get it over to you right away. In order to do that what I need to do is ask a couple of questions. Tell me..."

Sales Superstar

Thinks: *"It doesn't matter. Talking about it is much better anyway."*

Understands: Early on in a relationship clients will rarely read generic literature. What's worse is that if they do, they will often prejudge whether they want to do business with you or not. Building strong client relationships and new business is about people not about paper!

Why this works

• Takes responsibility for the situation • *"Right away"* implies urgency

• Links to needs based questions

———————————

YOUR NOTES

"I need to speak with other decision-makers."

What client means

"I need more time to decide" or *"I lied to you about being the decision maker."*

This is a pretty good objection for clients, as salespeople just don't know what to say to it. If it is true then what can you do? If it's not how can you call the client a liar?!

Average salesperson

Thinks: *"Liar! Liar! Pants are on fire!"*

Action: Tries to push to expose or pressurise the client. Whilst this will occasionally work its clearly not a great strategy!

——————————————

YOUR NOTES

"That's fine. It's certainly crucial that an important investment like this one is fully supported. In order that I can give you all of the support you need and answer any questions they may have I'd like to ask a few questions. Tell me, how many other..."

Sales Superstar

Thinks: *"How do I get this moving again?"* **Understands:** Whatever the truth is here the important thing is to rebuild rapport, regain trust and agree a way forward. If there's a hidden objection the Sales Superstar will find it.

Why this works

• Respects the client's position and reframes thinking to *"important investment"*

• Everyone likes *"support"* if offered correctly

• Questions about the others involved "smokes out" hidden objections and decision-making strategies

• If it's true that there are other decision-makers then you can start to construct an action plan

---

YOUR NOTES

"Call me at the end of the week."

What client means

"Go away for now."

This client is either too busy to talk right now and wants to talk to you later in the week or they are hopeful that they will be able to avoid you in the future. There could well be a hidden objection here.

Average salesperson

Thinks: *"Yes. OK."*

Action: Agrees to call back and exits the call leaving control of the relationship firmly in the hands of the client.

———————————

YOUR NOTES

"Thanks for asking me to. When in the week would be best for you? Thursday or Friday?

AM or PM, which would be best?

3 or 4 PM?"

(And then confirm call time to client)

Sales superstar

Thinks: *"You're not getting away that easily!"* **Understands:** Average salespeople handicap their potential with unqualified and irrelevant leads. Working this unpromising pipeline restricts the time that they have available for identifying quality clients.

Why this works

- Sets up a qualified call worthy of your pipeline
- 95% of clients will ask you what the call's regarding allowing you to continue the call now with their permission

——————————————

YOUR NOTES

"Are you serious?"

What client means

"Not another sales call!"

This objection is nothing more than "bluster" and has no real substance. Ironically, emotionally based objections are often amongst the most challenging for sales people having a bad day!

Average salesperson

Thinks: *"No, I'm worthless. Why do I bother with this job?"*

Actions: Becomes defensive, verging on the aggressive. Needless to say – the call's going nowhere fast!

YOUR NOTES

"Yes, I am."

(Takes a breath for impact and then continues with call).

Sales Superstar

Thinks: *"Yes. Totally."*

Understands: Clients can't buy off every salesperson they meet as no client could possibly have that many needs. Most salespeople will back off at this type of objection. Ignoring it will put our Sales Superstar in the top 10% of salespeople before they even start selling!

Why this works

- Answers the question
- Psychologically takes control and passes the message that this call is important enough to take seriously
- Moves elegantly back to your planned call structure

——————————————

YOUR NOTES

"You can't help me!"

What client means

"I don't want to speak with you."

This client has made a decision not to speak to you based purely upon the fact that you are a salesperson.

Average salesperson

Thinks: *"Why is everyone I call so rude?"*

Action: Feels rejected (again), pitches his product desperately and ends up reinforcing the client's original opinion.

———————————————

YOUR NOTES

"Oh, I'm sorry! Many of my other clients thought that too before they saw the benefits of what we do. I'm sure you have good reasons for saying that – do you mind me asking what they are?"

Sales Superstar

Thinks: *"How can I turn this around?"* **Understands:** This client is only objecting to the sales call in general not to you personally. Once you've built professional rapport this objection will probably disappear.

Why this works

- The apology takes ownership and is unexpected
- Breaking the client's pattern here is important
- It acknowledges that the client has reasons for his opinion
- The question then starts a conversation and digs for any real objections

——————————————

YOUR NOTES

"I'll take it if you discount!"

What client means

"I think I can get a deal here!"

In this situation the client thinks that they have the upper hand. Past experience will lead them to believe that salespeople will always discount to get the deal.

Average salesperson

Thinks: *"Oh, please don't let me lose it now!"*

Action: Starts to worry and allows the fear of loss to cloud his better judgement and negotiating skills.

———————————————

YOUR NOTES

"I'm pleased that you have made your decision and I understand that return on investment is important to you, however you have secured our best discount already. When are you looking to receive the product / get started?"

Sales Superstar

Thinks: *"I know you want it anyway!"* **Understands:** This client wants the product or solution and this is an attempt to do a deal. Chances are that this is not a serious negotiation. If it is then it's the Sales Superstar's job to help the client to attach more value to the investment.

Why this works

- *"Decision"* implies something that is decided already
- *"Secured"* is an ego-flattering word
- Moves to a question which, if answered, presupposes the deal is done
- If the client is serious about negotiating then this is a "strong" starting position

---

YOUR NOTES

"Is this negotiable?"

What client means

"Have I got the best price?"

Clients have found that this seemingly unassuming question sends many salespeople into free-fall offering silly discounts! Wouldn't you try it if it worked most times too?

Average salesperson

Thinks: *"Oh no! I can't lose it now! How much can I discount this by?"*

Action: Moves into negotiations too quickly or even worse offers a huge discount. Ironically, this can lose the deal altogether due to the unstated message to the client about the low value of the product / service or the perception that the original price was too high.

———————————

YOUR NOTES

"Yes, of course it is. How much more do you want to pay?

(Client laughs or sounds shocked – breaking their pattern. Now slow down and speak genuinely...)

No, seriously ... you have already secured our best discount. When would you be looking to accept delivery?"

Sales Superstar

Thinks: *"Not likely. It's worth every penny!"* **Understands:** This client wants to buy and is now discussing terms. The balance of power has changed. It's up to the Sales Superstar to maintain the value of the proposition.

Why this works

• Answers the question and breaks the "let's negotiate" pattern by injecting humour

• Uncovers the times when you do have to negotiate for real

• Moves to a close using the presupposition that the deal is done

———————————

YOUR NOTES

"How long will this proposed meeting take?"

Client means

"Maybe but I'm not sure."

This client has not made up their mind about having a meeting with you yet and is going to make their decision based upon your response.

Average salesperson

Thinks: *"I can't believe it! Just when I thought I'd got it!"*

Action: Makes excuses, downgrades the importance of the meeting by reducing the time needed, talks rubbish and blows the meeting!

——————————————

YOUR NOTES

"That's a great question and I understand that we both need to get maximum benefit from the meeting. In order to do that, I estimate that the meeting will take about an hour depending upon how many questions that you have for me. Tell me, who else (is there anyone else) within your organisation (who) may benefit from taking part in this meeting?"

Sales Superstar

Thinks: *"See you at the meeting!"* **Understands:** This client sees the value in a meeting but needs confirmation that you won't be wasting their time. This is done through the psychological message (tone, pace, pitch, timbre etc.) not through verbal persuasion.

Why this works

• Acknowledges that both parties need to get maximum benefit from the meeting (this puts you on your client's level)

• Psychologically appears to put responsibility for the timing of the meeting into your client's hands

• In answering the *"who else"* question the client accepts that the meeting is taking place

———————————

YOUR NOTES

"We're not reviewing our suppliers at the moment. Can you send some literature so that we can consider you next time?"

What client means

"Not for you anyway! Go away!"

Most clients are keen to get you into their "process" for approval as it gets you off the phone in exchange for the future promise of consideration for supply! Once this "consideration" is given, most average salespeople are too scared to push any more for fear of it reflecting badly on their chances of selection!

Average salesperson

Thinks: "I'll find out when they are due to review their suppliers, send some literature and call back then."

Action: Takes time and effort preparing paperwork and calling back – usually pointless.

——————————————

YOUR NOTES

"That's fine because I wouldn't ask you to change now as I understand that forming strong supplier relationships is all about long term partnerships, profitability and return on investment. I believe that business is built on relationships and I would still like to invest the time now in getting to know and you and your business. Tell me..."

Sales Superstar

Thinks: *"But you might be soon!"*

Understands: Clients review their suppliers all of the time and are often economic with the truth about the "real" processes. Clients also regularly buy from outside of their listed suppliers to meet specific needs.

Why this works

- Agrees with the client position
- Demonstrates your understanding of business partnerships at a decision making level
- Very few people don't want to get to know you
- Ignores second objection about sending literature altogether!

YOUR NOTES

"You're not big enough. We only deal with larger suppliers!"

What client means

"I don't want to know. Go away!"

This objection works wonders for clients as the hidden put down *("we only work with larger suppliers")* strikes straight to the ego of most salespeople. Also, it may well be true that they do have such a policy.

Average salesperson

Thinks: *"Why do I work for such a useless company?"*

Actions:

1) Bails out of the call feeling bad and adding to his negativity, or

2) Becomes defensive and starts to "argue" with the client as to why he should use him!

——————————————

YOUR NOTES

"It's certainly true that we're not the largest supplier in the market place although we do work with many of the key players such as ... (name clients). Tell me, (name client), what's important to you about dealing with large suppliers?"

Sales Superstar

Thinks: *"Then it's my job to help you to understand the benefits of working with a smaller supplier!"*

Understands: This objection is probably just an excuse. If it is a real objection the Sales Superstar needs to uncover the factors that helped the client to come to this decision in the first place. By understanding these factors he will be able to help the client to reassess that process and potentially come to a different decision.

Why this works

• Agrees with the client's position and makes a power statement about his own clients

• Positive language *"not the largest supplier"* is psychologically better than "small"!

• *"What's important?"* digs out the original deciding factors and enables the Sales Superstar to reposition his solution to match them

—————————————

YOUR NOTES

Six Simple Strategies That Will Handle Any Objection!

Strategy 1 - Don't Fan Fires!

When I was a young lad I used to love going on school camp. One of the most exciting things about camp was getting to cook your own food on an open flame. I remember the first time we had a go at it and we built this massive fire to cook our fantastic feast on. Unfortunately, all we managed to do was incinerate the bacon and eggs within seconds!

One of the teachers came over to us and explained that it was all about controlling the flames not stoking them up!

When I run seminars and programmes I am constantly amazed by how even quite senior salespeople manage to fan really quite minor objections into raging infernos with a combination of their own perceptions, emotions and reactions. When you take the time to control your emotions and reaction you can really start to control the fire.

With cold calling in particular many of the opening objections given by clients are merely bluster and have no substance behind them whatsoever. Even when they do have some substance (e.g. *"we use another supplier"*) they don't necessarily require an answer right away. Acknowledging the objection and moving on is sometimes all that is required at this stage.

Unless there is any particular reason why, I will normally approach most first objections in a cold call in this manner!

Objections:

"We have no budget..."

"We have no need..."

"We use another supplier..."

"We have a preferred supplier's list..."

"It's nearly the end of the financial year..." "It's not my decision..."

"I need to speak to someone else..."

Answer:

"**That's fine**. The reason for my call is to..." Or, and if you really must say more...

"That's fine. I wouldn't expect it to

be any other way. The reason for my call is to..."

———————————————

YOUR NOTES

Strategy 2 – People Buy People So

Sell on Relationships!

People buy people. If everything else were equal wouldn't you buy from the person that you liked the best? Of course you would and so do your clients. This may seem obvious but it is a fact that's often overlooked by most salespeople. This is a shame because it's a fact that we can use to great advantage when selling.

Most clients are worried that you are going to push something onto them that they don't want. Why? Because we've all experienced salespeople in our lives who do this. By focusing on the relationship and not on the sale you start to put your clients more at ease. This allows them to stop worrying that they are about to get "pitched".

When I teach this simple technique to delegates and they get on the phones and try it they are always amazed at just how effective it really is.

Objections:

"We've got no need..."

"We've got no budget..."

"It's the end of the financial year..." "It's not my decision..."

"You need to speak to someone else..."

The "Building Relationships" Answer:

"That's fine. At this point most of my competitors would ask you when you do have a budget and arrange to call you back then. We at ... (name company) ... believe that business is built on relationships and I would still like to invest the time in getting to know you now. Tell me John, how...?"

——————————————

YOUR NOTES

Strategy 3 – People Like to Be Complemented

This principle is a little similar to the last approach and is based on the fact that most clients expect you to confront their objections, head on. By using this approach you avoid any confrontation and disarm your client because it is not what he is expecting. Importantly, you also differentiate yourself from the competition.

Objections:

"We have an existing supplier..."

"We use in-house solutions..."

"We farm that out to the states..."

"We have an internal person in charge of that area..."

"We use your competitors (ABC etc)..."

Answer:

"That's fine. I wouldn't expect it to be any other way. Many of my other clients said that before they became aware of how what we do complements what they are already doing. What I'd like to do is come down and see you / ask a couple of questions..."

———————————————

YOUR NOTES

Strategy 4 – Feel, Felt, Found

"I understand the way that you feel. Other people felt that way too. What they found was that..."

(Write your own feel, felt, found with a real case study in the space below...)

——————————————

YOUR NOTES

Strategy 5 – Respect People's Reasons

When I am selling I know that the majority of people who have a need for my services will already be getting something similar somewhere else. They will also have gone to some time and effort to find and select their current suppliers. Depending on the product I am selling, changing suppliers may be really quite difficult for the client in terms of time, logistics, cost, related systems etc. Clients are not sitting around waiting for a call from me so that they can change suppliers when I call them!

In fact, I don't want it to be that easy at all! If it was, anybody could call my clients and get an opportunity! I don't want clients that give everything out to anybody who rings them! I want clients with whom I can build meaningful and long- lasting business relationships.

It always amazes me that most salespeople want to turn around these kinds of objections with just one call. It shows a total lack of understanding of the client, their needs, or indeed of how clients really use our products. What kind of message does this kind of behaviour send to your clients about your business awareness?

The way to deal with this kind of situation is to take the time to understand your client's reasons and situation more fully.

Objections:

"We have existing suppliers..."

"We have preferred supplier's list..." "We do this in-house..."

"We contract this out..."

"This is controlled by the US..."

Answer:

"Thanks for sharing that with me and I wouldn't expect it to be any other way (I'm pleased that you take this area of your business so seriously). I'm sure that you had good business reasons for putting that in place. Do you mind me asking, what were they?"

(And ask as if you mean to get an answer!)

YOUR NOTES

Strategy 6 - Stepping Stones

Clients tell you what you need to know. Their words are like cement and you are the water. The question is ... Are you going to build a stepping stone or a weight to drown yourself with?

With stepping stones we leverage the client's own words to create a platform from which we can move towards our desired outcome. This is particularly effective when setting meetings but can be used in many ways. Read the examples below and then read **"Real Conversations"** for more detailed examples of Stepping Stones.

What is a Stepping-Stone?

Your questions

+ client answer

+ "that's exactly why..." + because".

You can use this pretty much anywhere, see opposite...

Example 1:

You: "I'm sure that you have good reasons for not doing sales training. Do you mind me asking, what were they?"

Client: "Well, it's too expensive and last time I didn't get results."

You: "John, I can see that would create questions and queries and that's exactly why we need to meet." (Close)

Example 2:

You: "I'd still like to invest in getting to know you. Tell me John, what size team do you have down there?"

Client: "Oh, about 60."

You: "How many of them are involved face to

face with clients?" **Client:** "Most of them I guess."

You: *"You know that's exactly why we need to meet because..."* (Note in this example that the word because is about to link to reasons why the meeting would be good.)

Example 3:

Client: "I've heard bad stuff about your industry. It's too expensive."

You: "I've heard that said too but it really doesn't reflect the return on investment that many of our clients have been getting and that's exactly why we need to meet..."

The Three As to crush common sales objections

There's three steps to crushing common sales objections.

Agree.

Address.

Advance.

Agree with the prospect

Address their issue

Advance them through the closing

Don't overthink it.

Just try these and watch them work.

Simple 10 objections cheat-sheet

I'd like to speak with my partner

"Speaking with your partner is a great idea. However, I highly doubt they will be as excited to talk about it as you are. After all, you're here. They aren't. I'm right in front of you and able to answer all YOUR questions right now, not theirs. Here's what I suggest you do. Let's go ahead and get you signed up and taken care of. You're here. Let's not waste any more time shopping. In the event your partner throws a fit and totally shoots down your proposal, you can simply return the item tomorrow. The only catch is if your partner wants the refund, ask him to come in with you to collect it. I got your back to make sure you get what you need."

——————————————

YOUR NOTES

I'm just not ready to make a decision yet

"I agree 100% that making a decision takes preparation. That's what I'm here to do for you. Prepare you to make a decision. We both know you need the product. You like it. It solves your problem. The longer you go without making a decision, the longer you'll have this problem. Let me help you. Sign here."

———————————————

YOUR NOTES

It's too expensive

"I agree it costs more than what you came in prepared to spend. We both know you don't want a cheap product though. Cheap products don't solve problems. The key is not how much my product costs, but how much getting the solution to your problem is worth to you. There's no such thing as a solution to a problem being too expensive. There's only those who aren't willing to do what it takes to get the problem solved. I'm ready to do what it takes for you. Are you ready to do what it takes for yourself? Let's do this!"

YOUR NOTES

I'll have to come back tomorrow

"I completely understand you are running short on time. You've come here, spent your time with me and now have to go. Coming back tomorrow only takes more of your time, though. You can spend a few extra minutes with me now, and get this over with, then instead of spending more time with me tomorrow, you can use that time to make up for the few extra minutes it takes to do this deal right now. Let's go. You ready?"

——————————————

YOUR NOTES

I need to shop your competitors to make sure I'm getting the best deal

"I understand that you want the best deal. We all do! There's nothing wrong with that. We can easily do a quick Google search if you'd like, and you'll see our prices are the same or better than anyone else. I'll meet or beat whatever is out there. What I care about is you. I want you to be happy and glad you decided to business with me. I assure you the deal on the table is way more than fair, if it's not the best. Let's close this up, move forward and let me show you why people love doing business with me."

———————————

YOUR NOTES

Let me think about it

"I agree you need to consider all the options before pulling the trigger. That's completely normal. Here's the thing though; I know you've been thinking about this for a lot longer than you've been here. You've thought about this a lot. That's why you showed up today. You want my product. It does exactly what you need. You just want to make sure it's the right decision. I get it and let me assure you with 100% certainty that it is the best decision for you. Thinking about this another day, week, or month, won't change the fact that you need this and want it. Let's just get you what you want and need. Sign here."

——————————————

YOUR NOTES

I wasn't prepared to buy today

I agree with you on being prepared before you make a buying decision. No one wants to be sold on something before they need it. When we were talking earlier, you said this was exactly what you needed. I'm not sure how long you've been putting your needs off, but that's never a good thing. Whether you buy today or a year from now, you're going to end up buying. Why wait any longer than absolutely necessary, to solve your problem and fill your needs? Let's get this over with and get you all fixed up."

——————————————

YOUR NOTES

I've got to go home and do some research first

"I agree with you that research is an important step to making a buying decision. Lemme ask you, though. Have you done any research before you contacted me? I'm sure you have, and I'd be willing to bet you know a lot more than you're letting me on to believe. And that's ok. I get that you can be leery of sales people. I'm here to assure you with product, service and satisfaction, that you're making the right decision and getting exactly what you need. Let's wrap this deal up."

———————————

YOUR NOTES

I can get it cheaper online

"I agree that online can sometimes be a less expensive place to purchase this. However, online takes the human element out of the equation. That means if you have questions, a problem comes up, or you need to return the item, it's all up to you. On top of that, what most people don't know is that most items sold for less online are scratch and dent. There's a reason they sell them for less, and I assure you it's not because they don't like making money. My price is fair, and my service and support come along with the package. Let me help you make the most of the product. Let's wrap this up."

————————————

YOUR NOTES

I don't have time today

"I agree that we are running low on time here. You've invested a lot of time into this. Time on research, travel, thinking and now with me. You told me this was exactly what you wanted today. You are out of time. And I think we can both agree you've already spent lots of time. Since you're out of time, let's wrap this up now and you'll never have to worry about the time dealing with this problem again."

____

YOUR NOTES

Sales Objection: "It Costs Too Much"

This four-step process will help you overcome price objections:

Step One: After the prospect has finished speaking, pause for three to five seconds.

(Hit the "Mute" button if you need to.)

Step Two: Explore the pricing objection. You can ask up to three questions before responding to the objection.

Step Three: Summarize their price objection in a few sentences.

Step Four: Circle back to your product's value.

Here's an example:

Prospect: "We really like the product, but it costs too much."

Rep: *Silence.*

Prospect: "The other options we're exploring are 10-15% cheaper. Is there any way you can come down a bit?"

Rep: "I understand. In fact, I had two other customers just like you who were uneasy about the price at first. But what they found was … "

The following responses to pricing objections allow you to acknowledge your prospect's concern without immediately slashing your price or causing them to walk away.

1) "Too expensive compared to what?"

"Expensive" is a relative term. If you can find out what the prospect is comparing your product or service to, you can more precisely differentiate value.

————————————

YOUR NOTES

2) "Really? How are you coming to the conclusion [product] is too expensive?"

This prompts the prospect to break down their reasoning. Once a salesperson better understands the specific concerns behind the sticker shock, they can more easily address them.

———————————————

YOUR NOTES

3) "Are there some boxes we left unchecked?"

Circle back and make sure the sales process unfolded to both parties' expectations.

———————————————

YOUR NOTES

4) "I hear you. The best products are often more expensive."

"a price objection isn't 'real' until the customer has brought it up twice."

Using this response the first time you hear "it's too expensive" can help you separate the prospects who truly don't have the budget from those who are merely kicking the tires.

—————————————

YOUR NOTES

5) "How much will it cost you to do nothing?"

Get them to think about the bigger picture. Reveal the hidden costs in the status quo.

YOUR NOTES

6) "Is it a cash flow issue, or a budget issue?"

This question gets to the heart of whether they are asking for a discount (budget) or payment terms (cash flow). Once the rep categorizes the objection, they can negotiate more effectively.

———————————

YOUR NOTES

7) "Let's explore some creative strategies for fitting this into your budget."

If your prospect doesn't have enough allocated funding, try to find a workaround. Suppose their department has a set budget for software and a separate one dedicated to maintenance. Instead of charging them one flat price, you might send one contract for your product and another for your service fees. Now that you've unbundled or unpackaged your solution, your prospect can fit it into the budget.

You can also bill the buyer in stages. Let's say your product would max out their quarterly budget -- and they need to save money for other purchases. Charge them half now, and half next quarter.

Not only will the buyer appreciate your flexibility, but you'll rescue the deal without compromising on price.

—————————————

YOUR NOTES

8) "Let's say money was no object. Would our product/service help solve your problem?"

A fast track back to value.

———————————————

YOUR NOTES

9) "What's too expensive?"

Asking this (gently) prompts the prospect to explain their conception of your product/service. Hearing a response along the lines of "Well, it's a lot for just X, Y, and Z" reveals their low value perception.

YOUR NOTES

10) "Too expensive? That's concerning."

Concerning because this product/service is so valuable for the cost. Nudge the prospect back to value.

YOUR NOTES

11) "Is price the only thing that's keeping you from signing?"

If the prospect has any other objections the salesperson needs to address, this question will surface them.

———————————

YOUR NOTES

12) "Okay. So which part don't you want?"

What you're telling the buyer is that price is inextricably linked to value. So if a buyer doesn't want to pay full price, they won't be able to get the full value. This question might prompt them to reconsider.

———————————————

YOUR NOTES

13) "Will price keep you from getting what you really want?"

You're not calling them cheap outright, but you are raising the question in their minds. And no one likes to be cheap, especially when their business is on the line. Alternatively, this will reveal if your product or service isn't the ideal solution for their problem.

——————————————

YOUR NOTES

14) "Does this mean we will never have the chance to work together?"

The word "never" is the kicker.

"When it comes to handling sales objections, 'never' is the most powerful word in the English language.

"Most people hate it. As a result, the vast majority of prospects will respond by saying, 'well, no ... not *never*!'"

The salesperson can then probe into the conditions required in order to strike a deal and adapt terms or walk away accordingly.

YOUR NOTES

15) "Setting price aside, do we have the product/service you want to buy?"

If they say yes, you can follow up with #12. If they say no, determine if it makes sense to go back to value or abandon the deal.

——————————————

YOUR NOTES

16) "What's the ROI you're looking to see?"

This steers them away from thinking in terms of "expensive" or "cheap," and towards the long-term value for their business.

———————————————

YOUR NOTES

17) "It might seem expensive for one day, but let's break it down by month/quarter."

A lump sum can seem scary to anyone. Have figures on how the cost distributes over years, months, or days at the ready.

——————————————

YOUR NOTES

17) "Is what you're saying that our prices are high in comparison to our competitors'?"

If your price is indeed higher than the competition's, this question opens the door for the salesperson to differentiate on value.

YOUR NOTES

19) "Have you ever bought a similar product or service before?"

Another possibility is that the prospect has an inaccurate idea of what this type of product or service costs -- perhaps because they've never purchased it before. With this question, you can clear up their misconception.

——————————————

YOUR NOTES

20) "Price is an important consideration. So I have some context: How much research have you done on what a typical investment is for a product/service like this?"

The question behind this one is, "Do you already know what something like this should cost?"

Thanks to your prospect's inexperience, they might be placing your product in the wrong category.

For instance, maybe your solution has both a data storage and an analytics component. If they compare it to other data storage options, it'll look significantly more expensive. But if they benchmark it with analytics software, your price is right in line with the competition.

——————————————

YOUR NOTES

21) "You think it costs too much?"

Feeding their line back to them forces the prospect to explain their position, and might make them reconsider in the process.

YOUR NOTES

22) "When's the last time you bought something based on price alone?"

Again, no one likes to feel cheap.

———————————————

YOUR NOTES

23) "I understand. In fact, I had two other customers just like you who were uneasy about the price at first. But what they found was ... "

Empathize with the prospect, and then address their concerns with a strong case study that proves value.

YOUR NOTES

24) "In your own business, is your product/service always the least expensive option available?"

If you're a B2B salesperson, this is a great line to have in your back pocket. The buyer's organization has to win deals too, and they probably do it on value and not just price. If delivered correctly, this line might elicit a chuckle -- and a signed contract.

YOUR NOTES

25) "Do you really need to say 'no' to our price right now?"

Seems a little harsh, right? Not so according to Tom Reilly, the sales expert behind this approach.

"When the buyer says, 'I don't know. The price is higher than I want to go,' try two or three ways to deal with it. If nothing works, offer this response and watch the expression on the buyer's face,"

"I guarantee they will raise their eyebrows."

If the buyer replies that they don't have to say no right now, the salesperson can then suggest the prospect take a few days to mull over the price -- and realize that by saying no the price, they're saying no to the product and its associated value.

——————————————

YOUR NOTES

26) "[Silence]"

Sometimes the best response is no response. When a salesperson simply falls silent after an objection, the prospect often begins to explain their rationale. The rep can then address specific concerns from there -- no prompting needed.

———————————

YOUR NOTES

27) "Compared to a candy bar, it's a significant purchase. But when we look at [weekly, monthly, yearly] ROI, you'll actually save money."

This light-hearted response helps you put your product in context.

____

YOUR NOTES

28) "[Prospect's name], I would rather apologize for the price today than for the lack of quality and your unhappiness forever. Now, let's not let a few dollars keep us from doing business together."

It reminds your prospect skimping on price will hurt them in the long run.

——————————————

YOUR NOTES

Real Conversations

These three conversations are excerpts from conversations that my delegates have had after training. Most of the conversations that I have chosen are ones where they were closing for a meeting. This is because they have no industry specific questions in them and are therefore applicable to any sales situation. It is a simple matter to close in the same manner to the next set of questions...

Conversation 1: The Easy One!

Sales: "... I'm sure there may be areas in which we can work together. In order to find out what benefits we may be able to add what I'd like to do is come and see you..."

Client: *"Is this a cold call?"* (Emotional objection)

Sales: "Yes. The reason for my call is to introduce myself and my organisation and to set up a meeting with you." (Answers with a simple "Yes" and moves on).

Client: "Can't you send me literature first?" (Standard client response)

Sales: "Yes, I certainly can send you literature first. However, our literature is pretty generic so what I'd rather do is come down and see you and then I can tailor the literature to suit your exact needs." (Derivation of standard literature approach)

Client: "I'm really not sure. I'm quite busy at the moment." (Thinking about the meeting)

Sales: "That's fine John. I'm quite busy too. I wasn't thinking for at least 4-6 weeks. How's your diary looking at the end of January, say the 24th or the 25th. Which would be better for you?"

(Acknowledges objection and picks up on the *"at the moment"* comment by positioning himself as busy too. Moves straight to an alternative close in the future)

Client: *"Hmm. Neither of those are that good."* (By implication, the client is now accepting the meeting, just not on these dates)

Sales: "When would be better then?" (Open question)

Client: "The following week I guess, towards the end?"

Sales: "Thursday or Friday John?"

Client: "Friday."

Salesperson sets up the meeting.

Conversation 2: No Need!

Client: "Can I stop you there. We have no need for sales coaching at the moment."

Sales: "That's fine. The reason for the call was purely to introduce myself and my company and to organise a meeting with you. What we do is work with companies like yours to help them to increase sales and maximise profitability. I'm sure that there are areas where we may be able to help you. In order to do that what I'd like to do is come and see you." (Answered simply with "that's fine" and then moved back to the planned suggestion of a meeting)

Client: "I just don't have the time at the moment." (Standard time objection again)

Sales: "John, I won't waste a moment of your time. I'm very busy too so I was thinking towards the end of January. How's the 24th or 25th looking to you?" (Simple answer, agrees that they're both busy, links to a slightly different diary close)

Client: "*Well that would be alright but I just don't see the need at this time.*" (A ha! Client has nominally agreed to the meeting but the *"need"* objection has come back)

Sales: "That's fine. Many of my competitors would ask you when you are going to have a need and arrange to call you then. I believe that business is built on relationships and I'd still like to invest the time in getting to know you. Which of those two dates would you prefer, the 24th or the 25th?" (Agrees and then uses the stock "relationships" approach. Closes straight out on the two dates as the client has already nominally agreed to them)

Client: *"Probably the 24th. Is this going to take a long time?"* (Client agreeing to the meeting but still wriggling a bit. His real concern here is not the meeting but the potential that it may go on too long!)

Sales: "No, it won't. To get the most value from the meeting I expect about an hour but that really depends on how many questions that you have for me. What time on the 24th would be best?" (Answers with a simple "No", introduces the value concept and then throws the responsibility to the client by linking the length of the meeting to how many questions the client has. Closes to a specific time on the 24th!)

Client: "Well about 4pm I think but I really don't have a need at this time." (One final check that he won't be bullied!)

Sales: *"That's fine John. See you on the 24th at 4pm."* (Chooses to confirm meeting confidently having judged that this would be enough to reassure the client)

Closes off with meeting!

Conversation 3: The Existing Supplier

Client: "I think that I had better stop you there. I

am totally happy with my current suppliers."

Sales: "That's fine. The reason for the call was merely to set up a meeting to explore areas of mutual interest. How's your diary looking towards the back end of January, say the 24th or the 25th? Which would be better for you?" (Bearing in mind that the objection was not even a question all the salesperson has to do is acknowledge and close)

Client: "Well, I'm always busy but I just don't see any point in getting together as I'm not looking to change suppliers?"

Sales: "That's fine. I'm not asking you to change now merely have a look at what we're involved with. We've worked with several of the major players in the market place to help them to increase revenues and maximise profitability. Like you, I'm very busy. I'm sure that there would be some mutual benefit in getting together. When you look at those days, which would be the more suitable, the 24th or the 25th?" (Acknowledges again but this time gives a bit more. Note the embedded commands and the controlled close "when you look at those days")

Client: "The 24th but I don't see any point. I'm happy with my suppliers. I really don't want to change."

Sales: "John, I'm not asking you to change, merely to agree to a meeting. Building the correct supplier relationships is essential to any business and I'm sure that you had great reasons for working with your current suppliers. Do you mind me asking, what were they?" (Agrees again, uses a link statement and then moves to understanding the situation better. Note this is the start of using a Stepping Stone)

Client: "No, of course not. We used to use a lot of suppliers but we found that we were not getting the levels of service that we needed. We need to be able to control our suppliers and get maximum benefits from them."

Sales: "Service is certainly an important aspect of any relationship – what are the critical elements that you look for?" (Questioning to understand)

Client: "Our operation down here is massive. We have 5 sites and 1000 employees. We're shipping kit out at least twice a day. Some of our clients need to be able to phone up, order and receive delivery within 48 hours. We can't hold enough stock to do this so we need a fast and reliable service from our suppliers." (Stating needs now)

Sales: "Sounds like you're pretty busy down there. How much stock are you ordering in a typical week then?" (Pacing and leading)

Client: "It all depends, several thousand pieces. It's a handful for any supplier." (A ha!)

Sales: "I suppose that it must be. What kind of challenges do you get?" (Not leaping in too fast!)

Client: "Not a lot but when they do occur it's mostly just around the fact that it's difficult for any one supplier to cover the changes in our stock usage."

Sales: "John, that's exactly why I'd like to come and see you because we've worked with several of your competitors in helping them to secure a fast and reliable service with total flexibility. I'm sure what we do could really complement your existing suppliers as regards to your changing stock usage. What time on the 24th would be the best for you?" (Uses the Stepping Stone and links the "because" to the client's own needs and in his own words. Clever use of "complements" too and then a simple close)

Client: "Oh, I guess sometime in the morning."

Closes out for the meeting.

The Assumptive Close

What's the assumptive close? It's a manipulative sales tactic where you act like the prospect has already decided.

Here are three examples:

- *"When should we get started on implementation?"*
- "What delivery date would you like?"
- *"Which [package, tier, bundle] are you going with?"*

Is this the worst way to close a deal? No. If someone isn't going to buy, the assumptive close won't get them to do a 180 -- so it's not as though you're tricking people into handing over their credit cards. You might, however, convince an on-the-fence prospect to walk away. This technique makes you come across as pushy and self-serving, which isn't the best impression to give when kicking off a business partnership.

Instead of this strategy, try these closing phrases. We promise they're more effective (and they won't make you feel like a slimeball).

Asking for the Sale

Use these non-aggressive closing questions to make the buyer feel comfortable -- without completely taking off the pressure.

1) "Is there any reason, if we gave you the product at this price, that you wouldn't do business with our company?"

This one turns salespeople into Jedi mind trick masters. In an Inc. article, Geoffrey James pointed out that if the prospect answers "no" to this question, the rep has indirectly gotten them to agree to the contract. If the answer is "yes," however, the rep has the opportunity to address objections without bringing the deal to a halt.

———————————

YOUR NOTES

2) "If we could find a way to deal with [objection], would you sign the contract on [set period in time]?"

Objections often kill deals. But in this case, handling the objection is actually a way of closing the sale. Of course, this depends on the company's ability to resolve the problem by a given date. But if a fix is possible, getting the customer to commit ahead of time is a clever way of turning a con into a pro.

—————————————

YOUR NOTES

3) "It seems like [product] is a good fit for [company]. What do you think?"

This question automatically makes your prospect think of all the reasons they're interested in buying. Because you end by asking for their opinion, it sounds genuine rather than self-serving. And once they say something like, *"Yeah, I think it could really help us with X,"* you've got the perfect segue into *"Great, I'll send over the proposal right now."*

YOUR NOTES

4) "Would you like my help?"

It's sort of perfect: gentle and friendly without being obscure or weak. Plus, it enforces the rep's image as an advisor rather than a hard-closing salesperson.

———————————

YOUR NOTES

5) "If we throw in [freebie], would that convince you to sign the contract today?"

Clearly, this closing technique isn't appropriate for every situation (it's called "selling," after all, not "giving away"). But for important or very large deals, offering an exclusive or time-sensitive add-on to sweeten the pot might be a smart move. Price discounts could also make sense in competitive markets. However, it's up to management whether they empower reps to make discount or freebie offers on their own.

YOUR NOTES

6) "Taking all of your requirements and desires into consideration, I think these two products would work best for you. Would you like to go with [X] or [Y]?"

The rationale behind giving two alternatives is that the prospect will be more inclined to choose one than turn both away (a third option that's been discreetly taken off the table). The rep thus increases their chances of hearing a "yes" to something rather than a "no" to everything.

YOUR NOTES

7) "I'd hate to see [negative consequence] befall your company because you didn't have the right product in place. Do you want to take the crucial step to protecting your organization today?"

Fear is a powerful motivator. This closing tactic is most effective in situations where the consequences of not buying will actually harm the business, instead of simply allowing the status quo to continue. It's best to pair this line with external factors, such as new legislation or economic conditions, which prospects can't control.

———————————————

YOUR NOTES

8) "Why don't you give it/us a try?"

It sounds so simple, doesn't it? The disarming and unassuming quality of this question is precisely why sales expert recommends it. Phrasing the decision as "giving the product a chance" instead of "making a commitment" downplays the risk and ramps up the rapport.

YOUR NOTES

9) "If you sign the contract today, I can guarantee we can do [special request the buyer asked for]. How does that sound?"

Similar to #2, but with one important caveat. The closing question in #2 assumes that the salesperson will resolve a prospect objection *before* they sign the contract. This closing technique-- called a "rebound close" -- promises that the rep will grant a special request *after* the prospect provides their John Hancock. This critical change in the closing timeframe reflects the difference between a deal-killing objection (that other vendors might be able to address) and a special favor (that other vendors will likely be similarly hesitant to grant).

———————————————

YOUR NOTES

10) "I know you said you need to have a solution in place by [date]. Working backward from that day and factoring in implementation and training time, it looks like we'd need to have a signed contract by [date] in order to meet that deadline. Can you commit to that signing date?"

If you know the prospect has a firm deadline they need to stick to, use it to crank up the urgency. And since you're using the prospect's deadline instead of pulling one out of thin air, this type of reminder-slash-closing line actually helps the buyer instead of unduly pressuring them.

YOUR NOTES

11) "Will you commit to doing business with us today?"

Ah, the old direct ask. Sometimes the simplest closing technique can be best, but other times it can come off as presumptive or pushy. A salesperson has to have a firm command of the situation and a high level of familiarity with their buyer to use this closing line successfully.

YOUR NOTES

12) "Ready to move forward? I can send over the contract right now."

Everyone likes the idea of progress. If prospects associate the purchase with forward momentum, they'll be likelier to commit. This closing line also reduces the friction of buying -- the contract is already ready, so all they need to do is sign.

————————————

YOUR NOTES

13) "You're interested in X and Y features, right? If we get started today, you'll be up and running by [date]."

Salespeople can encourage their prospects to make a decision by reminding them the sooner they act, the sooner they'll have their new system. Mentioning specific parts of the product doesn't hurt, either -- buyers will immediately start picturing how much easier their life will be with the new solution.

____

YOUR NOTES

14) "What happens next?"

"Whenever your prospect begins stalling or providing any other excuse for not acting today, you simply reply with (these) three words." It might seem crazy to put your prospect in the driver's seat like this -- but something's preventing them from buying, and you need to figure it out if you want any shot of getting their business.

———————————————

YOUR NOTES

How to Close a Sale

Want a more assertive approach? Try these closing lines.

1) "Unless you have any more questions or concerns, I think we're ready to get started."

You're leaving the door open for them to get more information while making it clear where you stand. If you've done your job surfacing and resolving objections throughout the sales process, the buyer will answer with something like, *"No, I'm good. I think we're ready too."*

———————————

YOUR NOTES

2)"Let's discuss pricing."

With this statement, you transition the conversation from general, abstract topics like ROI and product features into the actual agreement. It's not a very subtle shift, but it works.

YOUR NOTES

3) "Tell me your thoughts."

To gauge how ready your prospect is, say this. If they're looking for the metaphorical pen to sign on the dotted line, they'll usually say so. If they're still unsure, you'll hear some hemming and hawing. This gives you the chance to figure out what's holding them back without trying to close too soon.

———————————

YOUR NOTES

4) "We can take as long as you'd like, but I know [you've got another meeting at X time, this call is scheduled to wrap up in Y minutes]. With that in mind, maybe we should move to the actual agreement."

While you don't want to rush your prospect too much, reminding them of the ticking clock gives you a good reason to bring up pricing. Notice this response is framed around their schedule. If they want to continue the conversation you're currently having, you can offer to arrange another meeting.

Final Thoughts

No matter what else we're talking about in seminars, workshops and coaching sessions, I'm always asked the same question:

How do I deal with price resistance?

Price often is not the heart of the issue but an indicator that something else is going on. Clients will use the price objection because it's a convenient excuse.

A lot of the time, however, price is not the only issue and it's merely being used as a smoke screen. You are getting price pressure for a lot of the usual suspects that you already know—the buyer believes that they should push for lower price, uncreative people want more for less and so on.

I want to challenge you to think of price in a different way. If you are not offering a commodity, price is a by-product of other issues. You must be clear on these issues with the prospect or client so you can get control of the price discussion.

Don't respond right away. Instead, get the prospect to talk more about the objection. Ask, "And what else is of concern?" This does a couple of things: first, it allows you to get all the objections out at once. By doing this you get a more complete picture of what's really going on and can respond accordingly. And second, it gives you some time to think about how you want to respond. It's our tendency to jump in right away, respond to the objection, and move on. But you need to take your time and get the prospect to talk more about it so you can get to the heart of the issue.

Don't introduce price too early in the conversation. Price objections often come when you give the price too soon. Before you can talk about price in the sales process, you have to get the prospect to see the value and get them to articulate the value of the solution. When you share the price too early in the conversation you lose control. You move into the negotiation phase where all conversations going forward are going to focus around price instead of value and outcomes.

Focus on selling the value. When you get a price objection, you haven't done a good enough job of selling the value. Go back to the prospect's needs and goals. Get them to articulate what the solution is worth to them. When you get the prospect to see the value of the solution and you put it in financial terms, you get much less resistance on the price.My answer is easy when price is the only issue. Present the buyer with the lowest price option and win the deal.

Price is relative to business problems. If you are selling in the iron-triangle of Service, Quality and Price, then you are not selling value that solves business problems. You are selling into a comparative matrix that boxes you into a same: same measurement with our competitors. When you solve business problems – Time, Money and Risk—then you are in a very different dialogue. An example of this comes from one of my clients. They sell programming services on a particular operating system. This typically means that they are being compared on a bid with other vendors by how many hours it takes to complete the job and what the hourly rate is. In other words, they are a commodity in that market. However, they changed the conversation by saying the following:

"If you need this project completed in a year, anyone in our industry can do the work. If you need this completed in 6 months, we can give you a list of 5 firms that can do this work. If you need this completed in less than three months...we're it."

By defining the business problem as a time problem, price became a smaller part of the discussion. The interesting thing is that for those companies for which time was not the major driver, my client was still able to win business at their price because an important value of time and ability to finish the project with confidence was elevated in the conversation. The issue for all of us is how we frame the business problem apart from price.

Price is a reflection of confidence in outcome. If there were a 100% guarantee that there would be a resolution to a buyer's business issue, then his or her willingness to pay that price could go up. When I get price resistance on my proposals, I ask this question, "If we could get you a $20 million increase in sales in one year, would it be worth a million dollar investment?" Their answer is almost always yes. Then I say, "Well, this discussion is not about price then. It is really about your confidence in the outcome of this proposal. So, let's talk about what would give you greater confidence in this proposal and also let's make certain that all of your concerns are on the table." In responding to price resistance on large account sales, focus on the issues of confidence before you discuss price or terms.

Price is a reflection of measurement context. In the world of business solutions, there is no such thing as a true "apples to apples" comparison. Complex solutions are almost never exactly the same in the solution architecture between two competing companies. That means that there is no valid comparison between you and your competitor in the area of price. I recently used the example that you would not ask a nurse to remove a tumor, or a neurosurgeon to cure a cold. On the spectrum of care, these represent the same industry, but different problems and different solutions. This happens to you as well. A lower quality provider in your market is held up as "just as good as your solution" by your prospect, so therefore the only point of comparison must be price, right? Only if you allow it to be.

Never Haggle. The difference between negotiating and haggling is simple. Negotiating is when you are making adjustments in terms, conditions and scope of work between two parties. Haggling is when you are asked to do the same work as you have proposed, but for less money, period. I don't believe in haggling. If your work is priced correctly, then any adjustment in price will require an appropriate adjustment in scope, terms or conditions.

In my experience, the price resistance comes when no better context has been established for the discussion. Establishing the right context for the evaluation of your proposal is 100% our responsibility. If you are getting price resistance and your offering is not a commodity, then the context needs to be adjusted.

Online access, Workshops and Electronic tools

This book comes with online tools to support your sales and close deals. It include video recording and different tools.

It may provide Two complementary passes to our signature workshop on Sales and Closing Deals. Email info@winyourbrand.com to inquire about the list of cities and schedule of this workshop.

To access these tools email a copy of your receipt to info@WinYourBrand.com

About the Author:

Wael Badawy (Business Leader of Tomorrow and top 40 under 40 in business) is an international speaker, author, educator, innovator, and trainer. He successfully built seven multi-million dollar sustainable businesses within six months or less.

A tri-language speaker lectured more than 1.5 million entrepreneurs, business leaders, students and scientist on technology, innovation, business, and entrepreneurship. He has more than 60,000hrs of teaching, lecturing and keynote speech in business, engineering, technical, legal, arbitration, dispute resolutions and life transformation. He taught size of groups from 6 students to 14,000+ students in a single session. His audiences include world leaders, business owners, entrepreneurs, graduates, masters, seamen, community leaders, new employees, engineers, scientist, doctors, etc. Wael is a consultant; coach and trainer founded the Entrepreneurship Driving License and certified 17,000+ entrepreneurs in the first year alone, who used his strategies to build their businesses. Wael founded 23 international companies and operations sized from $1Million to $128Million, led eight National entrepreneurship initiatives and programs. Wael received at least 73 international awards, contributed 18 books and proceeding, 21 patents, 600+ peer-reviewed papers, and publications.

Wael Badawy is honored with two PhD in Engineering, three MSc in Science and Engineering, BSc (Honor), an MBA, and six Diplomas in International Laws and Arbitration.

He is a registered Professional Engineer in Alberta, Canada and Egypt, CMC member, CAPS professional Member, Senior Member of IEEE and ACM, SPIE, Fellow of The Phi Beta Delta Honor Society, The Upsilon Pi Epsilon Honor Society (UPE) and The Phi Kappa Phi Honor Society, among others.

A husband and father were looking forward to sharing with you his experience and transform your business, life, and future.

ISBN 978-1-989040-01-0 Electronic book
978-1-989040-00-3 Paperback

Printed in Poland
by Amazon Fulfillment
Poland Sp. z o.o., Wrocław

13495280R00197